About the Author...

Born near Findhorn, Scotland, of mixed parentage, S.D. Anugyan has worked as a microbiology technician, a science teacher and - now - as a Feng Shui consultant. His extensive travel and study of the world's most mysterious and sacred sites, as well as direct experience, led him to extend the boundaries of traditional Feng Shui and create a new approach - Radical Feng Shui.

He publishes the quarterly emagazine *Dragons, Tigers and Kookaburras*. For subscription details, and more about topics related to this book, visit
www.treetongue.co.uk.

To contact the author directly:
pager (UK only): 07663 788215
email: **radicalFS@yahoo.co.uk**

The Poisoned Dragon

Healing with Feng Shui and Geomancy

S D Anugyan

Tree Tongue

Published by Tree Tongue
2 Chapel Downs Cottages,
Threshers, Crediton, Devon. EX17 3PB
www.treetongue.co.uk

ISBN 0-9546099-0-5

To Salix babylonica

Contents

Photographs and Drawings

Photographs, drawings and other images are credited in the caption. Where no credit is given, the photograph is by the author.

The photographs which precede each chapter are by Premgit. Further details about his photography can be found by visiting his website at www.premgit.co.uk

Acknowledgements

Danu, Ian, Molly and Spike provided unconditional support right at the start.

Frances and Sig were also an important part of the journey.

Jennie and Prabhat gave invaluable advice on the Five Elements.

The numerous artists and photographers who contributed so much of their time and talent are named; but the others who gave in a different way, by generously sharing their stories and case histories, have had their names changed unless they requested otherwise.

Jenny for the final piece of the puzzle on the Morchard Bishop line and the chance to explore so much of the area on horseback.

Taranga for such beautiful and carefully chosen words.

Jon Kane Houldsworth - thanks for the picture, hope it's OK that we used it.

My thanks are due to all of the above plus many, many more.

The wise eagle that wants to see tomorrow's brightest day must be brave enough to shake the great reptile of the past awake.

- African saying

Introduction

Early Steps

My interest in Feng Shui began at a time when it was difficult getting literature on the subject. Consequently, my teacher was not a School, a Master or books, but the environment itself.

The actual first time I experienced anything relating to ch'i - the ubiquitous lifeforce that is perceived as being present in everything - in any way relating to the earth was when driving in Devon one day.

I felt something behind me. It was as if someone had actually touched the back of my neck. I stopped the car and looked around to see a solitary standing stone in a field. It had clearly wanted my attention.

I was a science teacher when this happened. I had been aware of talk about ley lines but had dismissed most of it as New Age entertainment. Not that I didn't believe in them, it was just that I didn't see any indisputable proof one way or the other; I had remained open to the possibility of their existence but that was it. This is actually the true meaning of scepticism, which tends often to be confused with prejudice or bias.

The experience with the stone marked the beginning of the end of my disinterest towards such matters. Around this time somebody lent me the book 'The Sun and the Serpent' by Hamish Miller and Paul Broadhurst. The book was about the authors' tracking of the famous St Michael alignment in England, starting in Cornwall and finishing in Norfolk. The lending of this book coincided with a few days' holiday I had, when I was intending to drive from Devon down to Cornwall, so I decided to visit a few places talked about in the book - though I still hadn't actually read it.

Armed with compass, a very rough map and the book, I set off one Sunday to Brent Tor on Dartmoor, one of the places on the St Michael line. That cold, sunny day I stood at the top of this high hill, by the little St Michael's church, and looked West towards Cornwall. In the distance I could see another hill and, inbetween, to my surprise, the sun glistening on various stretches of water that appeared to be in an approximate alignment. These were not lakes but ponds and various spontaneous gatherings of water after recent rain. Still, the coincidence of their following the St Michael line was quite striking.

I went down to my car and proceeded to drive West. I didn't use the map, I only had a few names of places from the book and a compass. It was an extraordinary journey, one that cannot be described easily due to its irrational nature. All along I met with bizarre concidences that kept putting me on the right route, to the next step on the line, such as a waitress approaching me in a cafe, telling me where to go next, having observed the book on my table.

That night as I lay in a hotel room on the Cornish coast I knew my life had changed irrevocably. I no longer saw things in the same way for I could perceive patterns in the landcape which had previously remained hidden to me.

Not that I abandoned rationalism entirely. On the contrary, it was to prove extremely valuable over the following years as I sought to understand the different areas of South-West England; and, as I began to glean the hidden array of landscapes, Dartmoor and Exmoor became my most significant teachers.

I felt encouraged to seek alignments, using maps and fieldwork. I did this by instinct, not wanting to influence my research through reading other people's theories. My first area of research was where the standing stone had 'touched' the back of my neck - immediately I glanced at a map I saw that the stone was in a more-or-less direct alignment with two churches, a crossroads and concurrent with a valley just outside my house, all within six miles. Fate was to bring me even closer to this alignment, as to this day I go horseriding regularly past the stone.

I traced more alignments across varying areas and spent much time driving or walking along them. I became aware that each alignment had a very specific character, for lack of a better word, and not always a healthy one.

So not only did I become convinced that 'ley lines' definitely existed but also that human beings had to some extent been manipulating them in the past through standing stones and other means.

Of course, there was much written about all of this but I still opted for direct experience and research, refusing to consult any texts. This was not only in order that I wasn't swayed by other people's opinions but also because I was bothered by one thing:

Namely, that this was all very fascinating but it seemed to lead nowhere, for it wasn't practical. There were plenty of theories around but none of them, in my view, contributed to people's well-being in any measurable way.

Which is where Feng Shui came in.

At this time, around 1989, there were very few books available that I could find but I managed to get some and I started reading. Immediately it was apparent that there were a lot of contradictions in Feng Shui, many different systems - and systems within those systems.

Ironically, this conflict was to be resolved for me by my developing interest in other cultures' ways of understanding the environment, such as Vaastu Shastra in India, the Australian Aboriginal songlines and Native American medicine wheels. This interest coincided, fortunately, with a lot of travelling in my life.

From my research I realised that Feng Shui was indicative of a universal truth rather than one limited to Chinese beliefs and localities. It was to the credit of the ancient practitioners in China that they had devised ways of working with the environment that we would find so relevant today, in other parts of the world, with so many other forms of geomancy lost to us; yet I found it sad that very few practitioners worked with the lung mei - colloquially known in the West as 'ley lines' - for, in my growing experience, they were absolutely vital in providing the main keys to understanding an environment.

The lung mei or 'dragon veins' provide the main flow of ch'i into an environment. Early on I realised that if those veins were harmed in certain ways, even if on just one point, the effect was similar to that of poison entering the human bloodstream: no matter where the point of damage originated, the entire organism could become diseased.

Further along my journey, as well as learning from other ancient cultures, I found myself working with more contemporary professionals, such as architects, electricians, builders and interior designers. Once they realised I was not dogmatic in my approach they were more than willing to share the fruits of their hard-won experience. I learnt much from them, such as: Why interior slopes can be at 44 or 46 but never 45 degrees. (The latter angle apparently has an oppressive effect.) Why purple is not necessarily of the Fire element, as many in Feng Shui claim, but could also be Metal or Water, depending on whether it is of a hot (Fire), cool (Metal) or dark (Water) tone. How to reduce the magnetic fields by twisting wiring every 30cm. How to control air movement in a loft, water movement in a bathroom; that is, the Feng (Wind) and the Shui (Water), through basic energy-saving procedures.

I also found myself alongside acupuncturists and other healers. The former, in conversation, questioned the pedantic methods in Feng Shui for determining one's dominant element. I myself was uncomfortable with standard systems such as using the year of birth for the 'element profile'. Through learning more about Chinese healing I discovered a far more complex and wondrous - more sensitive, I felt - way of working. I was made aware of Seiki-Jutsu, a Japanese method of healing, which uses the lung mei directly in a house for individual healing sessions. Herbalists told me what plants to use, such as hyssop and rosemary in garden borders to heal rifts with neighbours.

The list goes on and the journey goes on. It is partly because the journey is not ended and never will end that I originally called this way of working 'Nomadic Feng Shui'. This still seems fitting because there is a lack of borders here, a sense of belonging to no one place in particular; yet paradoxically retaining a profound appreciation for every piece of land on this incredible planet.

In many ways I feel more of an affinity for the shamanic roots of Taoism than for some of its recent flowerings into modern day Feng Shui; but shamanism in general has become very much an in-word and has been absorbed into Western concepts to such an extent that it is sometimes reduced to an academic exercise, with piles of literature supporting hypothesis after hypothesis. This I wish to avoid in favour of a more experiential type of Feng Shui or geomancy. There are no cut and dry concepts here and no avoiding going out and living these pages rather than talking about them.

Here is an extract from Lao Tzu's 'Tao Te Ching' :

Others are clear and bright,
But I alone am dim and weak.
Others are sharp and clever,
But I alone am dull and stupid.
Oh, I drift like the waves of the sea,
Without direction, like the restless wind.

This book and what I now call 'Radical Feng Shui' is for those who are capable of understanding this. If the poisoned dragon of our environment is to be healed it is going to require an openness, humility and understanding that is vast, at times frightening, but always ultimately rewarding.

Chapter 1

Radical Feng Shui

The truth often sounds paradoxical.

- Lao Tzu

Breaking the Rules

Let's get immediately practical by examining a few case histories. Look at the following list and try to imagine what TWO things they might have in common:

- Jane's bed has its back against the same wall as the main entrance into the room. On both sides of the room there are wall-to-wall mirrors. Walls, ceiling and bed-covers are all light green.

- Deborah, in South Africa, lives in a house full of cats and trinkets in every corner. She is surrounded by clutter.

- Jorg and Gabrielle have a house in rural Switzerland. The main door is facing north-east.

- Eva and Rolf's house is dominated outside by a house on a hill to the right of theirs, if you stand looking out from the front door.

- Ellie's house in Mallorca faces a mountain. Behind the house is a drop of twenty metres.

- Ivor's house is on a triangular plot of land.

- Derek lives in an attic with only a step-ladder to get there.

This is an entirely unfair exercise! If you are familiar with Feng Shui you will recognise one thing that these examples have in common, but there is no way you could know the second.

The first thing is that all of these cases have textbook bad Feng Shui. But the second thing only I could know, which is that the people in all of these examples are perfectly happy in their environments and have been for some time.

Let's look at each one in turn.

- Jane's bed has its back against the same wall as the main entrance into the room. On both sides of the room there are wall-to-wall mirrors. Walls, ceiling and bed-covers are all light green.

  Having your back to the entrance of a room is considered an inferior position - you don't know, because you can't see, who's coming in. Also, one mirror in a bedroom is considered bad Feng Shui, let alone a room full of mirrors.

  In most cases I would agree that there is a lot wrong here. However, the trick is in the colour. Outside of Jane's room a beautiful forest is visible. The green of the room 'echoes' the colour, then does it some more with all the mirrors. The overall feeling is of being in a beautiful forest glade, encouraging you to rest no matter who comes in the room or how much ch'i is bouncing off the mirrors!

- Deborah, in South Africa, lives in a house full of cats and trinkets in every corner. She is surrounded by clutter.

  'Get rid of clutter' is considered one of the golden rules of Feng Shui and when I told Deborah to 'keep her clutter at all costs' she couldn't believe it. The reason was that as I walked around the house and the extensive garden, with cats emerging out of shadows and groves, there was a sense of something archetypal going on. Most of the trinkets were from North Africa and there were many Egyptian symbols inside and outside the house. Some people would argue that this was a case of a past life influencing the present one, but that didn't matter. The main thing was that Deborah was deeply in touch with these symbols and what they represented, albeit instinctively. They were part of the richness of existence for her and to insist on her parting with them would have been invasive, cruel and pointless. This wasn't clutter; this was very powerful, life-affirmative ch'i.

- Jorg and Gabrielle have a house in rural Switzerland. The main door is facing north-east.

  A north-east entrance is known as 'the devil's door' in classical Feng Shui, the south-west as the 'devil's back door'. You will often see entrances to Chinese buildings placed at an odd angle in order to avoid these two directions. I am also currently living in a north-east facing house and have experienced plenty of good fortune since being here.

We'll be looking at compass directions in depth later on. Again I will tantalise you by saying that Jorg and Gabrielle are very interested in spiritual matters and their work has gone very well for the twenty years they have been in this house.

.

• Eva and Rolf's house is dominated outside by a house on a hill to the right of theirs, if you stand looking out from the front door.

The right side of a house is known as the White Tiger in most Feng Shui systems. The White Tiger should always be controlled by the opposite, Green Dragon side to the left of the house, which must be larger and more dominant than the Tiger. To have the White Tiger in control is inviting disaster.

Eva and Rolf had studied Feng Shui and knew this before they bought the house. They went ahead with the purchase because, despite their knowledge, they trusted their gut instincts more. They were, in fact, practising what I call Radical Feng Shui but others may refer to it in this case simply as intuitive Feng Shui.

None of us can explain totally why it is all right like this - because in many cases this is not a healthy situation - but we know it is totally okay. My own feeling is that the White Tiger here has taken over the protective, supportive function of the Black Tortoise behind the house, giving the poor tortoise a rest! In the end, it doesn't matter because everything has worked out fine - as Eva and Rolf knew it would.

• Ellie's house in Mallorca faces a mountain. Behind the house is a drop of twenty metres.

This is similar to the last example, where the immediate surroundings to a house are not 'correct' Feng Shui. The back of the house, the Black Tortoise, where one expects support, is missing; and the front, the Red Phoenix, where one needs open space for the Phoenix of good fortune to fly out into the world, is blocked.

Ordinarily this might be a problem but this house is a meditation centre. The mountain to the front creates a feeling of inwardness, encouraging inhabitants to focus more on what's going on inside themselves rather than be distracted by the outside world. There are many ways to accomplish this with a building, but blocking the Phoenix is very effective!

The back of the house would still be a problem though if it weren't built like a fortress - there are no doors at the back and very few windows. The protection needed at the back is in the design of the house itself. Not a perfect solution, but it suffices.

- Ivor's house is on a triangular plot of land.

In both Feng Shui and Vaastu Shastra this is a disastrous situation, yet Ivor is very happy in his house and has been for some time. He wasn't even aware that the plot had this awkward triangular shape till I pointed it out to him. The secret is in the fact that the land is broken up into smaller segments by high hedges and flower beds, so that the triangular shape is not evident: thus, the experiencing of the land here by an individual is not 'triangular'.

- Derek lives in an attic with only a step-ladder to get there.

Step-ladders are often a problem in that the empty spaces between the rungs don't allow the ch'i to move up and down the steps. The usual precaution is to fill in the gaps or to encourage more ch'i by growing ivy up the ladder, trailing Christmas lights along its sides or lighting up the space beneath.

But Derek is a teenager. He actually wants to disconnect himself from the family, needing that space in which to do it without losing touch with them completely. Enough said!

These are just some examples where Feng Shui rules are broken and need to be broken.

Radical Feng Shui works more with guidelines than rules. It is necessary to state what some of those guidelines are, but before I do that it's necessary to take a step back and - without resurrecting more ancient history already available in other literature - look at the world of Feng Shui today in a general light.

Crystals and Dragons

Originally Feng Shui in China was a luxury that only the nobility could afford and what has survived today from those obscure origins is a discipline that is practically a marketable commodity, with all the inherent aggression one associates with the business world. The famous Bank of China in Hong Kong is in the shape of a cleaver 'cutting the competition'. Sarah Rossbach in her seminal book 'Feng Shui' tells the story of neighbours fighting back at each other's offending ch'i with an increasing armament of mirrors till the traffic is confused by the reflections and the police intervene. One often comes across an interview with a Feng Shui practitioner bad-mouthing others as conducting 'incorrect Feng Shui'. Practitioners in Imperial China were known as 'dragon men' but all this is a far cry from tracing dragon lines in the landscape and living in harmony with the environment.

There is a story by the American writer Ray Bradbury about two competing cities in ancient China: one city has its walls in the shape of an orange to signify wealth and abundance. The other city later builds its walls in the shape of a hungry pig to devour the orange. The first city, panic-stricken, rebuilds its walls in the shape of a stick with which to beat the pig. This goes on till both cities are almost destroyed by the ongoing effort to compete with each other. Eventually they act on advice to build one city's walls in the shape of the wind; the other, in the shape of a kite. The wind needs the kite to be visible in its glory, the kite needs the wind to fly. In this way both cities can prosper.

This is good advice that we could do with now.

People beginning to take an interest in Feng Shui for the first time are nearly always totally confused by the conflicting theories and methods. This is largely because of the two main types of Feng Shui available today:

Classical or **Traditional Feng Shui** - Composed of two main disciplines: The Form and Compass Schools. However, even within these schools are many different theories. Popular authors include Lillian Too, Derek Walters, Lam Kam Chuen, Man-Ho Kwok.

Black Hat, Modern or **Western Feng Shui** - Often derided by afficionados of the traditional schools, this is the Feng Shui normally adopted by New Age devotees. An important difference from the older methods is that the ba-gua - the octagonal template placed over maps of buildings and rooms - is oriented not according to compass directions but to main entrances. Popular authors include Sarah Rossbach, William Spear, Karen Kingston.

Whenever people ask me which methods I use I answer something like, 'All of them and none of them'. 'But which method is the true one?' I'm asked, to which I may paraphrase Buddha: 'Truth is that which works.'

It is absolutely essential to be adaptable, versatile. In this way it is possible to work in very different types of environment without imposing a pre-made set of rules on people. This is particularly important as one comes into contact with other cultures and other, sometimes very alien, environments: as we move into Space and the depths of the sea as a species it is clear that some old Feng Shui rules are inappropriate, if not downright ridiculous.

The Ba-Gua or Pa Kua

FORTUNATE BLESSINGS South-East Wood	ILLUMINATION South Fire	RELATIONSHIPS South-West Earth
ELDERS East Wood	TAI CHI Centre Earth	CREATIVITY AND CHILDREN West Metal
WISDOM North-East Earth	JOURNEY AND CAREER North Water	NETWORKING North-West Metal

⬆   ⬆   ⬆

In the black hat system the entrance is always from this direction.
Traditional systems use the compass directions shown within the grid.

Rules only appear to offer stability. Traditionalists in Feng Shui are quite hot on rules, which would imply that they are all 'of one mind'. This is not the case at all. The Compass systems themselves vary considerably. For example, one area a practitioner might look for in a house is the one called 'Five Ghosts'. I used different methods to work out where that was in my house once and ended up with so many ghosts it was a wonder that there was any room left for the living.

Attitudes to pyramids, particularly the famous glass pyramid by the Louvre in Paris, are very revealing as well. This is how three traditional practitioners respond to the shape:

> *'...The frightful glass pyramid at the Louvre reveals the unfortunate collaboration of the elements of both Fire and Water.'*
> (Derek Walters, The Feng Shui Handbook)

'It is a superb Fire structure, drawing down intense energy from the heavens...It is perfectly balanced with the Water structure of the Louvre.'

(Lam Kam Chuen, The Feng Shui Handbook)

'Pyramids were for the Pharoahs and thus more suitable for the dead than the living.'

(Lillian Too, The Complete Illustrated Guide to Feng Shui)

This is hilarious. At least, though, there is agreement that the Fire element is involved i.e. that the shape is sharp and pointy. The basic rule here is not in dispute, it is in its significance that opinions differ. My own view is that they are all right, that the universe is big enough to accommodate contradictions and paradoxes quite easily.

Not that it is just traditional practitioners who follow rules. Black Hat practitioners can have their own dogmas; for example, through a blind aherence to various areas in a room being worked on as the Wealth Corner, the Relationship Corner etc., at the cost of losing sight of the bigger picture. The ba-gua in any method is rarely more than ten per cent of the necessary work; sometimes it can be missed out altogether.

Having said this, I do have an enormous respect for the Black Hat system for one reason above all others: that reason is called yi.

It is difficult to translate the meaning of the word but in my experience it is often the single most important factor in Feng Shui.

The closest one can get to 'yi' in English would be something like 'intent'. But 'intent' is not quite right because it implies that what you are thinking of when conducting a Feng Shui session is important. This is only partially true, for yi comes from something that doesn't belong to your thoughts or your feelings. Nor you. 'Neti neti' is the Sanskrit phrase - 'Not this, not that.'

Yi is like the fire of the original source, your spirit.

One can also call it magic.

I went to a house one day and my clients informed me, 'It was really odd, but things started changing in the house immediately after we called you. And we haven't even done anything yet.'

Somebody else phoned me about an ex-client in London, a friend of theirs. 'When I look at how her life changed, it all started from the day you visited.'

'Did she do the main thing I told her to do?' I asked.

'No, but everything changed anyway.'

These are both examples of yi in action. In effect, it is very humbling because you realise how small as an individual you are - that there is something much larger than your little ego doing the work. At the most you are a vehicle or a catalyst for change to happen.

I sometimes think of it as a lit candle passing its flame to another, but that analogy is not entirely correct either as the second candle was already lit - it just didn't know it.

'You're just giving me an excuse to do what I really want to do,' said one client.

Yes, exactly. Not that it's always that simple, which is why books are written, surveys requested and Feng Shui consultants have a job.

Black Hat practitioners use various rituals quite often in their surveys, as do others. In a larger perspective this is just a means by which the yi can operate, rituals giving it a 'voice'. Native American rituals are very popular today and I often find them just as effective. A Christian exorcism theoretically works in the same manner. In this way it does come down to intent: it doesn't matter what words you use but what you mean by them.

It is to the credit of the Black Hat Sect that they have consciously recognised the importance of yi and given it the prominence it deserves. I take my hat off to them!

Here is an irreverent summary of the two main groups in Feng Shui today:

	Traditional Feng Shui	Black Hat Feng Shui
Politics	Republican/Conservative	Democrat/Labour
Brain	Left side dominant	Right side dominant
Computers	PC users	Mac users
Obsessed by	Numbers, arithmetic, crossword puzzles	Personal feelings, crystals, chanting
Client base	Business corporations	Seekers, drop-outs
Eating habits	Always eat at the same place at the table	Eat anywhere, preferably not using a table
Respect for	Anyone who's been to one of their trainings	Anyone with a pendulum
Common advice	'Knock down half the building'	'Paint a pretty picture on the bathroom door'

Divine Symmetry

The main principle of the Taj Mahal is not based on the flowing, meandering curves of a river so beloved in Taoist principles, but on symmetry. This is a recurring theme in Islamic art, symmetry being indicative of a divine order in a universe that seems to be full of chaos. The tradition from which this stems can be traced further back to Greek and Byzantine art plus others, at the heart of which is a sense of the divine unity of spirit.

Photograph: Premgit

Now that I've been rude to just about everybody, I want to take a more compassionate view of this.

In his philosophical book 'Crystal and Dragon', David Wade talks about what he perceives as two main forces in nature: the drive for a crystalline order and fluctuating, unpredictable movements of chaos.

Society often expresses itself in a need for order, symbolised by soldiers or bands marching with the individuals equidistant from each other, like the atoms of a crystal. This order can be enhanced through tradition, through ritual. The downside of this can be a sense of restriction, a lack of movement.

Movement then comes through the lashings of the dragon's tail, through revolution - whether of the spirit or as a political movement. The downside of the dragon forces is that nothing can be established healthily, therefore growth is impossible.

The crystalline and dragon forces are both needed in a cosmic duo, revealing a complexity and beauty that would not be possible with only one. The trick is recognising who is leading the dance at what time - but it always takes two to tango.

Both principles can manifest through any 'system' and inevitably will do, but it is the preference for one or the other that needs to be recognised. Islamic art, expressed through beautifully complex patterns, is representative of a need for order. The ability to 'read' when an order is creating problems is essential, but that doesn't mean it should be abandoned totally in favour of random, chaotic lines simulating the movement of water. Versailles in France suffered from the effect of straight lines pointed at the palace, creating 'killing ch'i' or 'poison arrows'.

Zen Bridge

Why are you in such a hurry? Unless used with great geometrical awareness and precision, straight lines are generally best avoided. Bridges such as this - by breaking up a too-linear route - encourage one to pause and take in the surroundings, be part of the moment.

Photograph: Ronald Jones

The White House in Washington is another famous example. The architects of Beijing, faced with the same problem, introduced kinks in the streets to break their horizontal straightness and steps at the sides to break the vertical lines.

Taoism, as reflected in its art, is more favourable to natural chaos. Lao Tzu was reluctant to even give statements regarding his teachings: 'The Tao that can be told is not the real Tao' is the first thing written in the 'Tao Te Ching'. Yet the formal teachings of Tai Chi, Feng Shui and many other related disciplines have very much encouraged Lao Tzu's teachings to persist to this day and age.

In life there is space for both crystalline order and regenerative chaos - as is hopefully demonstrated within these pages.

Specifics of Radical Feng Shui

For the crystal part of ourselves here is a summary of guidelines for Radical Feng Shui:

1. The lung mei - paths of concentrated ch'i in the earth - are extremely important. Any comprehensive understanding of a site has to take them into account.

2. Humility is vital. You approach a site, knowing that you are there to learn from it - not it from you.

3. An openness to other cultures and other methods is required.

4. All rules and guidelines change. Be aware of this and be prepared to adapt at any moment.

5. Be respectful of the fact that every individual is on a personal journey of discovery.

The dragon parts of ourselves will suspect that even the above criteria are likely to change and that the best advice is to follow one's gut-feeling, our intuition. Or maybe not.

Although each of the above will be covered in the following chapters, let's briefly examine them in turn first:

The Lung Mei

There is much written in books on 'Earth Mysteries' about ley lines, geomancy, power spots etc., not so much in books on Feng Shui. I am primarily interested here in looking at how the lung mei can have a tangible effect on an environment and how best to work with that. Some of my research and examples will confirm what has been said or known before, some will refute it.

No-one can claim to have a monopoly in understanding earth energies, quite the opposite. It is something that belongs to everyone. I have just been in the situation where I have had paying clients who needed answers that basic Feng Shui could not deal with. I was therefore forced to come up with 'that which worked'.

So I recommend scepticism towards what is in these pages. Read it, practise it and decide for yourself.

Humility

By this I simply mean the ability to learn, where Feng Shui is passive rather than active. Modern Feng Shui in particular betrays its bias through a visual emphasis. Eyes are very much an active, yang sensory system: 'He had a roving eye', 'That's your projection', 'Her eyes shot daggers'. We live in a visually dominant society and this is encouraged by the way Feng Shui practitioners sometimes utilise colours, art and light at the expense of what can be heard.

The ear is more yin, female. Individuals with a predominant auditory sense have a hard time in modern society. Indian temples built in the past according to the Vaastu Shastra system utilised various acoustic tricks through their architecture in ways we cannot replicate. Sound is a forgotten science. Even more recently, in the Christian era in Europe, some buildings such as the Dom in Aachen, Germany, have superb acoustics that we cannot emulate now. An attempt to built an exact copy of such a building (not the Dom) in Berlin failed entirely, though dimensions and material were precisely the same as the original.

Cheap materials in a modern building's construction allow sound to travel extensively between rooms, permitting no real privacy for individuals; ground and air traffic invade every built-up area; and the songs and sounds with which birds and animals communicate are eradicated by the constant hum on the perimeters of motorways, creating unnatural dead zones for the entire length of our busier roads. Silence is a dwindling commodity that estate agents can sell for exponentially increasing prices.

When I go to a site I sometimes just sit quietly for a while and don't do anything. I listen and I feel. I try and understand.

I apply this also with individuals. I listen not only to what they are saying, but to the sound of their voice. (More on this when we deal with the Five Elements.) In my mind I pretend I am 'walking a mile in their moccasins'.

Openness

The Feng Shui here is clearly not limited to its Chinese roots. It owes much to other cultures. The chapters on lung mei are particularly global in their influence, but compass directions and their meanings have come as much from Indian and

Native American cultures as the Chinese and the concluding chapter is derived largely from Western science. In practice - particularly with gardens - I often draw on the related Japanese art of fusui or on aesthetic tricks from Islamic design.

Connected with this is an individual's spiritual beliefs. It is important to respect their personal symbolism and to work within those parameters as much as possible. For example, one client placed two small replicas of church gargoyles above her bathroom door to deflect any ch'i that might be lost that way. I've known other people to put tarot cards or Om symbols on doors for the same reason.

Yet it is also important to stand outside personal bias and look with a child's eye: one person had a statue of a pair of Sumo wrestlers in her Marriage area, which she found beautiful but was causing havoc between her and her husband!

There is a point also at which cultural bias becomes absurd. Western buildings occasionally avoid the thirteenth floor because of the superstition around that number, so that the floors jump from twelve to fourteen. The Chinese have a similar fear around the number 'four' because in their language it sounds like 'death'. So we can skip out floor numbers four, thirteen - and nine as well because in English it sounds like the German for 'no'. International buildings can become a complicated affair. It is much more likely that healthy global evolution will have to build on individual cultural strengths rather than insular superstitions.

Guidelines

That is all they are - guidelines. Even if you call them rules. Above and beyond these guidelines is experience - and each individual's experience is unique.

Journeys

When working on somebody's house a Feng Shui practitioner is like a stepping stone. The client calls him or her at a particular point in their life, a point at which they obviously need some guidance. But Feng Shui is an ongoing process. Not only should it be responsive to the seasons - decorating with fresh flowers in the summer, dried twigs in the winter for example - but also to the changes in a person's life. This is so obvious it's hardly worth saying, but it is important that things evolve around us as life does. Traditional Feng Shui uses many calculations to determine what changes are appropriate at what times for individuals.

The lung mei fit into this as well, for the best method by far to understand the effect a line may be having on your home is to follow it. That in itself becomes an inner journey reflected by the outer.

Everyone has their own journey to make and ultimately it is made alone, but it is good to have company occasionally along the way.

Related Reading

Crystal and Dragon	David Wade	(Resurgence)
Feng Shui	Sarah Rossbach	(Rider)
Nada Brahma: The World is Sound		
	Joachim-Ernst Berendt	(East West)
The Power of Place	James A. Swan	(Gateway)
The Way of the Earth	T.C. McLuhan	(Touchstone)

Chapter 2

Wheels of Life

The opposite of a truth - is another truth.

- Saying of unknown origin

Too Many Directions

People beginning to take an interest in Feng Shui are often concerned that their house is 'wrong' according to the ideal site. This is particularly so if the main door is facing an apparently unfavourable direction.

Of all the compass directions you will probably hear the South mentioned the most often as being favourable in Feng Shui literature, with South-East being an acceptable alternative. The 'ideal house' faces South, has high hills to the rear (North) and hills flanking both sides, though the western side should be lower than the eastern.

The preference for southern views from a purely aesthetic perspective will be obvious - but only in the northern hemisphere. In the southern hemisphere, southern light is quite obviously not as desirable as the warmer light to the North. This is where the origins of Feng Shui become clearly limiting, though there are ways to adhere to the rules and still get the desired light, through conservatories at the rear of the house, for instance. There is a recurring idea that the rules for the southern hemisphere simply 'mirror' those of the northern - ie opposite rules apply - but I doubt that it's that simple. For instance, which rules would be relevant if you live on the equator? Hopefully this book will support you in being sensitive to the actual location you're working in and not imposing preset rules on it, particularly in regard to compass bearings.

Explanations vary for why certain directions are insisted on in Feng Shui, ranging from wind direction, magnetic lines, balance of yin and yang in light to cosmic rays.

Wind direction: Argument in the past has been put forward that it was the dust-carrying winds coming from Mongolia in the North-East that determined the unfavourable reputation of that direction in China. Obviously this then does not apply to other parts of the world, where winds such as the föhn from the Alps or the sirocco from Africa have adverse effects on areas and come from very different directions.

Magnetic lines: If the favourable and unfavourable directions in Feng Shui are derived from magnetic or any other type of force in the Earth itself then the rules are likely to apply to wherever you are in the world. However, what refutes this is that the favoured directions in Vaastu Shastra are often North and East, with the North-East area being of particular interest, which we will be looking at shortly, and South generally considered unfavourable. In addition to this, in some systems of Feng Shui, such as the Pa Che system, various directions, including the North-East, will be the most desired if the individual's birthdate supports that.

Cosmic rays: The summer solstice in the northern hemisphere has its sunrise in the North-East. Some researchers claim that this causes an excessive flooding of solar radiation from this direction. In accordance with this, the solstice in ancient China was considered an extremely dangerous time and the Dragon Boat Festival - practised in both China and Japan - would take people near water around this time, thus counteracting the excessive heat from the sun. Whether having a doorway in this direction would expose you to extra radiation though is questionable.

Demons: In European magic the North was often considered the home of demons. In Taoist magic it was the North-East, though this is not exactly true as it is more the direction of the last star in the handle of the Great Bear - Ursa Major - that is supposed to denote the direction of black magic - and this direction is constantly changing through the night. 'Demons' can be taken as indicative of a scientific truth - such as cosmic rays - as superstition or as symbolism of the darker side of ourselves. Or perhaps all of these.

Light balance: As this is the most obvious one for most of us it is worth looking at in more detail:

The Language of Light

Light speaks to us all the time and it is a language we understand very well though we may not have the words to describe it.

Cinematographers use it frequently, sometimes at the expense of the spoken word. Ridley Scott is a good example. In his science-fiction film 'Blade Runner' there is one scene in particular which is of relevance:

The main character visits the head of a large corporation near the beginning of the movie. He is shown into a large room. The light inside is low but through the huge windows at one end of the room can be seen the setting sun. It creates a strong, uncomfortable glare. The feeling is one of age and decay. Our hero asks that the blinds are drawn in order to pursue his work. In a short time the director has subliminally told us a lot about the various characters, the corporation and about the general situation on Earth. Novelists use a similar technique but require a lot more time - and words - to do it in.

It is unlikely that Ridley Scott knows about Feng Shui consciously but intuitively he does. The low glare of western sunlight is considered one of the most pernicious forms of sha in Feng Shui. In Hong Kong many corporations utilise blinds on their western windows so that the workers are not affected by this light.

Drivers too are uncomfortable with heading directly into this light: it seems to create an awkwardness, an irritability which, oddly enough, is not evident when the sun is rising in the East though the practical difficulties of driving towards the rising sun are much the same.

The setting sun can be seen differently in a different context. For example: romantically. The completion the setting sun symbolises could relate to two lovers who have completed one stage of their lives and are now ready to be together. Or it could symbolise the end of an era. Or, again, the end of life ie death.

But unless we wish to be in a continual state of completion we would not wish for this energy to be with us forever - we are likely to need the newness and the freshness of the East to keep us going. This correlates with the principle of two-thirds yang/one-third yin required in living situations - eastern light has obvious yang qualities and western light obvious yin qualities.

What about the other directions though? As already mentioned, some basic Feng Shui beliefs fall apart when confronted with working in the southern hemisphere, where the sun is in the northern sky. My examples herewith will, unfortunately, be limited mostly to the northern hemisphere.

The South therefore - in the northern hemisphere - will be where the sun reaches its zenith. Noon is the time of maximum light and therefore yang. Houses are often built facing the South for this reason though some are built facing South-East, thus ensuring that two sides of the house received maximum light rather than just one. This is also a favourable direction in Feng Shui as it combines the wisdom of the Green Dragon with the luck of the Red Phoenix (see below).

The northern sides of buildings receive no direct light, are much darker and softer in tone, therefore yin. Artists often favour this light to work in.

We are now ready to look at the four directions in Feng Shui terms.

The Feng Shui Zoo

The four cardinal points of the compass are divided thus:

East - The Green Dragon
Status: Mostly yang.
Associations: Wisdom, protection, freshness, vitality, spirituality.

South - The Red Phoenix
Status: Yang.
Associations: The World, luck, joy, hope, success, inspiration.

West - The White Tiger
Status: Mostly yin.
Associations: Protection, unpredictability, excitement, danger, violence.

North - The Black Tortoise
Status: Yin.
Associations: Mystery, nurture, security, sleep.

Looking at these beasts, one can understand why the 'ideal' Feng Shui house has the characteristics listed earlier. The Green Dragon needs to be stronger than the White Tiger, therefore with higher hills or higher buildings on that side; yet if the White Tiger is totally missing then there is a boredom, a lack of excitement inherent in the site. Balance needs to be retained but, generally, the Green Dragon should keep the White Tiger under control. They are, as is often stated, like two guardians of a building who need to work together.

The Black Tortoise at the North and the rear of the 'ideal' site needs its protective shell enhanced through something like high hills, trees or another building, while the Red Phoenix in front needs open space in which to fly. It was quite common for the Chinese to build artificial hills to the rear of their homes for the Tortoise and, recently, in Canada there has been controversy due to the Chinese community chopping down trees in front of their homes in order to permit good fortune to reach them via the Phoenix.

At this point the fallacy of expecting all buildings to adhere to the 'ideal' situation is quite obvious. Your own home is extremely unlikely to have all the qualities listed. So what do you do? The answer is in how we perceive a place. First of all, the directions even in traditional Feng Shui are no longer dependent on the compass, as we shall see; secondly, once we are freed from cultural limitations many more possibilities start to reveal themselves.

The Animals Uncaged

As you will discover by reading almost any Feng Shui book on the market, the four animals around a site tend to be determined today not so much by their compass directions as by their positions. This does not mean the above information regarding the position of the sun and the effects of light should be ignored. It is still immensely important and should be taken into consideration when assessing a site.

The animals are now determined thus:

Green Dragon: to the left of the house as you look out

White Tiger: to the right

Black Tortoise: at the back

Red Phoenix: in the front

Positions of the Four Animals

Drawing by Emma Jones

This quantum leap in the system is not easily justifiable rationally yet it seems to work. It is possible that these directions have something to do with their influence on the left/right sides of the brain. This could also explain why the Black Hat system for determining the ba-gua according to entrances works.

One of the joys with this system is that it is versatile; it can be applied not only in various parts of the world but on a smaller scale as well. For example, what you see in front of you when you work at a desk is your Red Phoenix; what you have behind is representative of your Black Tortoise. It is often the case that if the Black Tortoise is missing outside a house then this 'theme' is repeated inside, like an unconscious echo, where inhabitants sit or sleep. Once this is made clear and talked about, it can be changed.

Action:

Investigate where you: A. Work. B. Often sit. C. Sleep. At each place check the four animals mentioned above. Ask yourself questions such as:

- Is the Green Dragon (left) side or the White Tiger (right) side the strongest? How do you feel about that? Don't go by what you think you 'should' feel - stick to your truth.

- Is your Red Phoenix blocked or is it open? Are you facing a blank wall or something that gives you space to 'soar'? Would you like to change this? If so, how?

- Do you feel solid support behind you, in the Black Tortoise area? If not, and you want that sense of security, how can you improve matters?

Checking the meanings of these different directions should give you some idea of the forces you are creating in your day-to-day life. You can also look at the overall balance of yin and yang. For instance, if the Black Tortoise and White Tiger areas are generally the best-represented, that makes the yin very strong. In such a case, ask yourself how that feels and then decide if you want to change anything to improve matters eg by making the other - yang - areas stronger.

Some Tips:

- Computer monitors are normally best at the Green Dragon side of the desk ie the left. Ergonomically though, twisting your spine is not to be recommended, in which case you should extend your desk on the left so that you can face the computer directly.

- To create more excitement in your life, make the White Tiger stronger where you sleep or sit eg with a cupboard. This is usually best only for short periods because of the inherent dangers with the tiger.

- If you often sit with a window behind you, draw the curtains or pull down a blind to allow support from the Black Tortoise. If there is a doorway behind you, use an auditory signal such as chimes or bells to alert you when someone enters. Chimes should only be hit on their clapper by the door, not on their tubes. Make sure you like the sound!

- If there is a blank wall where you have your Red Phoenix, open it up by placing a picture there that contains a view in it, something you like to look at when you glance in that direction. You can also consider using a mirror, though not usually in a bedroom.

Medicine Wheel - A Holistic Approach

In order to question the overall rule of South being the best direction one only has to live in India for a while. Being nearer the equator than China, the heat in the summer there is unbearable. Shade is a much larger requisite than the rays of the sun; consequently, doorways are very likely to be facing North. This practical consideration echoes the secular architecture of Vaastu Shastra which often favours North, with sacred architecture favouring the East. Also, one notes, the pyramids at Giza in Egypt face North.

It seems that directions in any culture have both practical and symbolic significance. The question is whether there is any universal truth involved or whether it is cultural-specific.

Focusing on the symbolism for a while, I realised early on that the different directions enhanced different lifestyles. The emphasis in Feng Shui was on happy families and business success; in India the whole country seemed to be steeped in meditation, whether individuals practised it or not. The quiet tranquillity of the North supported this; and the rising of the sun in the East is clearly indicative of awakening, of spiritual enlightenment.

A picture was starting to reveal itself but I was left wondering whether the West direction - the White Tiger in Feng Shui - could also mean more than the 'death' association it normally had.

The answer came when somebody showed me a Native American Medicine Wheel. There are many types of Medicine Wheels but this one was very simple and clear with only the four cardinal directions drawn out. I was struck not only by the similarity of meaning with the different directions to the Chinese and Indian versions but also by the name for the West: Path of the Jaguar. Another big cat.

One meaning ascribed to this direction was 'Courage'.

With more research into various medicine wheels plus direct experience working on different houses some interesting conclusions could be reached:

- There are no good or bad directions. Every direction has something to give: a specific energy, advantage or life lesson.

- The names given to the directions are just that: names. They differ from culture to culture but what they represent often does not. What does vary is the culture's attitude to them.

- Often people are drawn to a specific direction because that is what they need at that time in their lives.

Having established all this as a basis, it is possible to draw up our own 'Medicine Compass'. This is designed according to the four cardinal directions and each of their mid-points - which is accurate enough for most purposes, though more directions and their associations are, of course, possible and exist in various cultures. In fact, it would be more accurate to say that many versions of Native American culture support seven cardinal directions rather than four - the centre being of immense importance - as it is also in Vaastu and Feng Shui - and the vertical directions of above and below. A compass, though, tends to work horizontally!

A further note regarding the southern hemisphere is necessary first. The meanings ascribed to directions here are not intended to implement yet another dogma. They are part of a tool that may or may not be useful. Most people living in the northern hemisphere almost certainly will find this useful. But as one moves nearer the equator and over it, things are likely to change regarding the North-South axis. This compass is one of the fruits of ten years working mostly in the northern hemisphere, whereas the amount of time I have spent with this in the South is much less. Consequently I feel unqualified to jump to conclusions and would wish to inspire others to do similar research in their locality.

Medicine Compass - Eight Directions: Their Meanings and Associations

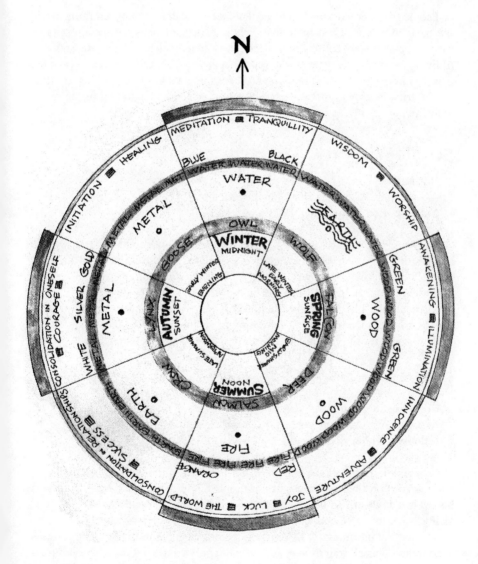

A modern-day compass for the Northern Hemisphere

Drawn by Hilary Johnson

EAST

Awakening, illumination.
Associations: Spring, dawn, the Wood element.
Colour: Green.

People living or working in a place that faces East are normally confronted with the need to 'wake up' in their lives. It is a rush of new energy and vitality, supporting any new ventures or projects. Any adherence to old patterns and ways of living are likely to create problems. A negative aspect of this direction is a tendency to never grow up, to remain naive, retaining a sort of 'puppy dog' energy.

The trick is to really treat each day as if it were 'the beginning of the rest of your life'.

SOUTH

Joy, luck.
Associations: Summer, noon, the Fire element.
Colours: Red, fiery orange, warm purples

People living or working in a place that faces South are encouraged to be successful in the world. The South is associated with Summer and therefore connected with the 'ripening of the crop'. This is a direction of happiness, sometimes known as 'the child'. The flip side of this direction is a superficiality, like children always playing in the shallows of the waters unaware of the oceanic depths, not so much naive as never daring to venture out into other realms.

Key words for the South could be simply 'Enjoy' and 'Celebrate'.

WEST

Consolidation, courage.
Associations: Autumn, sunset, the Metal element.
Colours: White, silver, gold

People living or working in a place that faces West are likely to be continually confronted with the 'truth' about things; and the ultimate truth for our physical bodies is that we are all going to die. Here is 'the skull beneath the skin': superficiality is not tolerated and any attachment to it will create problems. The trick is to be honest at all times: with yourself, the other people in the building, visitors, everything. This all sounds very serious but it only comes out that way because of our fears around truth-issues. In practice, West-facing buildings lead to very dynamic situations - yes, sometimes confrontational, but also very funny. And a sense of humour is very important here. One famous example of a highly successful West-oriented building is The Heritage, a home for the elderly in San Francisco. The direction is entirely suitable for its function and, as if to honour this, the bricks and terracotta edges alter colour beautifully with the late afternoon sun.

NORTH

Meditation, tranquillity.
Associations: Winter, midnight, the Water element.
Colours: Black, blue.

People living or working in a place that faces North are imbued with a sense of serenity no matter what their outer circumstances are. This direction, in opposing balance with the outer, yang qualities of the South, supports going inside: meditation. Particularly good for writers and artists, the North encourage passivity rather than activity. The downside is that inhabitants may become morose and isolated, particularly if they are resisting the urges to 'go within'.

Having established associations with the four cardinal directions it is possible to deduce meanings from the secondary directions, which are each a combination of their 'parents': These directions also relate to the Celtic 'cross-quarter days'.

SOUTH-EAST

Innocence, adventure.
Associations: Early summer, mid-morning, the Wood element
Colour: Green

It is not suprising that this is a favoured direction in Feng Shui, combining as it does the good fortune of the Red Phoenix with the wisdom required to deal with it effectively, from the Green Dragon.
People living or working in a place that faces South-East have the twin-influence of both innocence and experience. Not only do they have a strong visionary sense, they can act on it in the world. In fact, problems may persist if they attempt to shut themselves off from the world. 'No man is an island.'

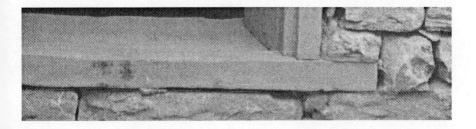

SOUTH-WEST

Success, consolidation.
Associations: Late summer, afternoon, the Earth element
Colours: Yellow, earthy oranges, tans

This is a combination of the success granted by the South with the wisdom of years as symbolised by the West. In practice this means that business success is only likely if combined with honesty and depth, superficiality not being tolerated; and, contrariwise, introspection or even romance is not likely unless tempered by remaining 'in the real world', that is, the physical world.

Problems are likely to occur if worldly success is emphasised without questioning what that success is actually for - or if less worldly concerns are insisted upon without making use of them. The Buddha must live in the marketplace!

NORTH-WEST

Initiation, karma.
Associations: Early winter, evening, the Metal element
Colours: White, silver, gold

People living or working in a place that faces the North-West may still be experiencing the dramas and confrontations that occur under the West influence, but they are also given more space in which to deal with them. The intervals in the Great Drama are becoming longer and more frequent. Truth is still insisted upon but in a much more gentle way now with the softer qualities of the North.

A strong drive to understand is paramount with a likely emphasis on spiritual concerns. But the introspection here is not as total as it is in the North; on the contrary, there is still very much an awareness that the world needs help. This is a very good direction for healers and visionaries.

NORTH-EAST

Wisdom, worship.
Associations: Late winter, early morning, the Earth element (traditionally)

The infamous 'devil's door' in Feng Shui! The seasonal assocation here is that of the dormant seed in the soil - Spring and warmth have not yet arrived but they are just around the corner. The long dark hours of Winter are over and the days are becoming longer. However, it is darkest before the dawn.

In Vaastu the North-East area of a house is known as 'Puja': worship. This is where any shrines or altars are likely to be placed and the direction itself is known as the Gateway to the Gods. In Feng Shui this is 'Gen': stillness, wisdom and the direction is treated as that of Earth (more on the Five Elements in the next chapter), with the associated colours of yellow and tan. Yet the Vaastu system recommends white, light yellow or light blue. My interpretation of this is that the Water element is so strong, North vitalised by the approaching forces of the East, that the Chinese chose to control it through the Earth element, whereas the Indians chose to express it (with a minimum of control from the light yellow). White marble is deemed especially favourable for the North-East in Vaastu whereas white (Metal) feeds and enhances Blue or Black (Water) in Feng Shui. You have to make up your own mind as to whether you feel you need to control this direction or go with it.

People living or working in a place that faces North-East are encouraged to be introspective but also to become aware of how they are going to utilise any wisdom they may gain from their introspection. Books are a good stepping-stone between meditation and the world, for instance, and the North-East encourages reading and writing and is generally good for creative people who need serenity in order to do their work.

It is fairly obvious why this direction might have the reputation it does. In Europe suicide levels are extremely high between Christmas and spring. The dark, brooding days and nights of winter juxtaposed with the hope of spring is a difficult combination when somebody does not actually envision hope as a reality in their world: springtime becomes a taunt rather than an optimism.

Meditation of some sort is perhaps even more essential for living with this direction than it is with the North.

The Building's Tone

Knowing the direction a building faces reveals the 'theme' or 'tone' that is ever-present inside. This will, of course, express variations depending on other factors, such as Five Elements and the lung mei, but by establishing the compass bearing of the entrance you will understand a lot about what is inside without even stepping through the front door.

Problems often arise when that direction is 'fought'. An example would be somebody trying to make money at the price of their 'soul' in a North-facing building; or, in contrast, somebody only interested in meditation in a South- facing house.

As always, rules can be broken, but in most cases it is likely that the above guidelines will prove correct

Those practising Feng Shui will be aware of the question recurring of where exactly the main entrance on a site actually is. There's no easy answer to this and experience is normally the best guide. For apartments, though, the most effective way usually is to use the main entrance into the building rather than that of a separate apartment, then balance it with the light-influences in the apartment itself. In some cases the secondary influences - such as the windows in the apartment - can seem to take precedence over the main door to the building. For example, a block of apartments may face West, with all the related energies affecting the inhabitants, but people in an apartment there with only East windows may be conscious more of the influence from the East than the West. The latter though will remain a constant and dominant, albeit more subtle, influence.

One factor that will determine the direction of a building could well be wind direction, as mentioned earlier. The wind to avoid could be the North-East and/or it could be the West - as it is in Devon and Cornwall in England - or another direction entirely, depending on where you are in the world. Effectively, in this way the environment is 'setting the tone' on a large scale as an entire area is likely to have several of its houses facing the direction most favoured in that locality.

As a footnote, being a person with more than a passing interest in some of the world's beaches and harbours, I have found the beach or harbour 'tone' also largely determined by the direction it faces. When you're next on holiday, experiment!

The House Axis

It is possible to think of the journey between the front and the back of a house as an 'axis', a symbolic version of the world axis. The latter, of course, is a North-South orientation and is represented symbolically in Europe by the Celtic Cross which is a combination of the world axis and the wheel of death-and-rebirth ie of cyclic renewal.

The axis within our houses is extremely important as it extends the dynamic established by the main entrance. We can 'play' with this to our own ends.

For example, if you have a North-facing house, the dominant tone created will be yin. This is one of the reasons that direction is avoided generally in Feng Shui, the desire, as stated earlier, being to establish a balance of approximately two-thirds yang, one-third yin. But our axis therefore will be North-South. This means that we can have our cake and eat it by building on the strengths of the South direction, thus retaining the sense of solitude characteristic of a North house but balancing it with the yang energy of the South. The way to do this is by allowing plenty of light in at the back, perhaps with a conservatory. In Australia sometimes people who wish to retain the original preferences of Feng Shui rules and build facing South, open up the backs of their houses to allow light in from the North - which is their way of bringing in more yang.

A client from a South American country once had the unusual request of seeking an explanation of why he ran into trouble a long time ago, with the militia seizing control of his business and all his assets, for he had done nothing wrong. He showed me the plans of his house whilst explaining that, his country being equatorial, the preference was often to build so that the front and back of a house were on an East-West axis. This, he informed me, was to gain the maximum benefit of light.

What was interesting in this case was that his house had faced West, with large windows at the back in the East. The dynamic therefore was one of confronting the truth - about himself, his business, everything - and if he didn't the result would have to be dramatic and 'difficult to miss', which was the West influence, resulting in greater understanding and more of a sense of his spiritual path, the East. This was exactly how it happened, for after he had lost everything he questioned his existence profoundly, became interested in spiritual matters and consequently regenerated his business with more wisdom and insight. The transformative powers of the West had done their job.

Related Reading

Amazing Scientific Basis of Feng Shui
        Dr Ong Hean-Tatt   (Synergy)

Earth Medicine	Kenneth Meadows	(Element)
Feng Shui Handbook	Lam Kam Chuen	(Gaia)
Vaastu	Rohit Arya	(Destiny)

Chapter 3

Elements

Physician, heal thyself

\- Luke 4:23

Elementary Background

An understanding of the Five Elements is an essential aspect of Feng Shui. It is one of the most difficult concepts for beginners to come to terms with, yet also extremely rewarding when they do. Part of the difficulty lies in the apparent contradictions of various systems, part of it in a confusion with the Western concept of four elements and part of it simply in the recognition of each of the elements - which is not always that simple.

We recognise the presence of various elements in a location through:

1. The shape or form of the landscape or building.

2. The material or colour.

The accompanying table (see over) and later photographs show the associations with each of the elements. For example, a tall building such as a skyscraper would be of the Wood element.

To understand the surrounding landscape, we would look at the shape of the hills perhaps or the dominant presence of a particular material e.g. a forest would be Wood, a lake would be Water. With surrounding hills we would concentrate more on their shape e.g. sharp, pointy crags would be Fire.

Each element describes a particular dynamic of ch'i. The easiest way to explain this would be to look at the seasons associated with the elements, something we have already started to do with the compass directions in the previous chapter. This particularly fits in with the fact that another word derived from the original Chinese for 'element' is 'phase' - therefore that the elements describe a continual process.

If you think of Wood as Spring you can imagine Wood energy as being growthful, expansive, bursting with energy. Fire as Summer is expressive, joyful. Earth requires a special mention, so we'll return to that in the next paragraph. Metal as Autumn is quietening, perhaps mournful. With Water as Winter, you can perceive it as being introspective, withdrawn.

Returning to the Earth element, it is a more complex affair than the other four. It is often seen as the 'season between seasons', or sometimes simply as Indian

Table of the Elements

	Shape	Colours	Season	Direction	Taste
Wood	Tall Columnar	Green	Spring	East	Sour
Fire	Sharp Pointed	Reds	Summer	South	Bitter Burned
Earth	Flat Cuboid	Yellow Tan	None	Centre South-West	Sweet
Metal	Round Circular	White Silver Gold	Autumn	West	Spicy
Water	Amorphous Irregular	Black Blue	Winter	North	Salty

Summer between Summer and Autumn. In terms of directions - for we have already looked at East being Wood, West being Metal etc. - Earth is seen as being in the North-East, South-West and central sectors of a building; though in the Black Hat system cardinal directions are ignored (see Ba Gua diagram on page 26).

Now that the association of the elements with the seasons is fairly clear we can see that there is a natural progression of the elements, echoing the seasons: Fire, as Summer, follows Wood as Spring etc.

This is called the Creative Cycle (see diagram opposite).

It is understood that each element generates the next. For instance, a weak presence of Fire could be enhanced by the presence of Wood, making the Fire stronger.

The other sequence shown is the Control or Destructive Cycle. This shows which element is controlled by which. For instance, if the Fire presence is too strong on a site it can be controlled by the Water element.

Putting all this together, a lot can be understood about the dynamics of a site just through looking at the elements involved. For example, skyscrapers are of the Wood element, as already stated. If those skyscrapers are next to an abundance of water, such as in Manhattan, this is part of the Creative Cycle - the Water nourishes the Wood. This is a harmonious situation, provided that the skyscrapers are supported by the Four Animals (see previous chapter).

If the skyscrapers are in an Earth location, such as the flat plains of Texas, the Wood of the buildings are controlling/dominating the Earth of the landscape. Houston in Texas, therefore, is in the position of power. But this is a short-term

Sounds	Organs	Emotions	Associations	
Shouting	Liver, eyes, gall bladder	Anger	Assertion, rules, organisation, vision	**Wood**
Laughter	Heart, Heart Protector	Joy Happiness	Celebration, openness, inspiration	**Fire**
Singing	Stomach, Spleen	Sympathy	Caring, earthiness, mental clarity	**Earth**
Weeping	Lungs, Large intestine	Grief	Richness, pragmatism, objectivity	**Metal**
Moaning	Kidneys, Bladder	Fear	Courage, reassuring, assessing risks	**Water**

Element Cycles

Creative Cycle

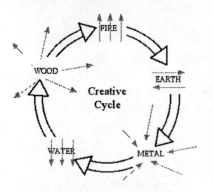

Fire burns to ash, nourishing
Earth which produces
Metal which catches
Water that feeds
Wood which feeds
Fire...

Control Cycle

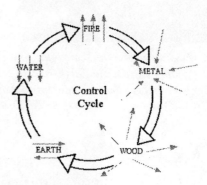

Fire melts
Metal which chops
Wood that draws the goodness from
Earth that dams or muddies
Water which puts out
Fire...

situation, good for quick profits but that's it. The Control Cycle, remember, is also known as the Destructive Cycle.

Determining which elements are involved is not always so straightforward. Although form takes precedence, sometimes the presence of a certain material can dominate a shape. Other complications arise frequently and the way in which a site is 'read' may vary between different people, as we saw even through the simple example of a pyramid-structure in the first chapter.

Experience is definitely the best teacher here.

Headington, Oxford

A Wood structure (tall, upright) in an Earth environment (flat). Wood 'draws the goodness from the Earth' and so this is a part of the Control or Destructive Cycle. Further disharmonies are likely from a total lack of support from the Green Dragon, Black Tortoise etc as detailed in the previous chapter.

Action

(You can do this now, after reading this chapter or later after having studied more on the Five Elements.)

Using the table for the Five Elements in Feng Shui (page 58), walk around where you live and check how well each of the elements are represented inside the building. Do this by awarding a point every time you observe the presence of an element, eg green walls would be one point for Wood, iron pots and pans a point for Metal, North-facing windows a point for Water etc. When you have finished, add them all up and note which elements seem best represented and which the worst. This is not, of course, an accurate measurement - it is merely designed to encourage more awareness towards the elements in your life. If there seems an imbalance in any element, don't panic for this might be perfectly all right for you. Give yourself time to understand more about that element's dynamic and decide how you feel about it. Act only when you really know what you want to do such as by bringing in a missing element, eg Metal through steel pots, through the colour white etc.

'You Don't Know Me'

Most people tend to know which animal they are in Chinese astrology, according to the year they were born. As a possible guide to individual characteristics, I have found all types of astrology useful to some extent, particularly when taken in a light-hearted manner; but also the tendency to label individuals - whether with a 'good' label or a 'bad' one - I find one of the greatest insults possible, for every individual human being is so unique and mysterious that ultimately they defy labelling.

A friend of mine was in Thailand visiting a renowned acupuncturist when she mentioned to him that she was a Tiger in Chinese astrology. "You're not a Tiger!" he yelled. "You're a Tree!"

This was an observation, based not on her year of birth, but on her demeanour. The healer's exclamation shook her out of her fixed idea of herself and started to open up more possibilities.

In traditional Feng Shui a practitioner will use a person's birthdate to determine their profile and any favourable alterations in their house or workplace.

This is one of the many places where I part company with traditional Feng Shui. I found this whole approach too dogmatic for my liking and started talking with acupuncturists about alternatives for working with people.

"How do Feng Shui practitioners work out the elements?" one healer asked me.

"They use the birthdate," I explained.

"Oh," she said quietly, obviously wondering how to be diplomatic about this state of affairs. "There are much more interesting ways to do it than that."

She was right. I read numerous books on Chinese Healing, talked with experienced acupuncturists and started to make my own observations with the people I met in the course of my work. What evolved out of this was an understanding and appreciation of individuals and their needs, enabling me to develop not so much a system as an awareness of the elements at play in various situations. I discovered a richness and freedom in this approach that had previously eluded me and which could be applied anywhere at any time.

The sections that follow outline a more personal approach to the Five Elements than is usual in Feng Shui. It is not necessarily meant to replace a Feng Shui system that you may already find successful, more to present an alternative way of looking at things. A way that many could find rewarding.

Healing Oneself

If you look at the table on page 58, you will notice the various associations of emotions and different organs of the body with the Five Elements. It is clear that we each have all of the elements within us - for example, we all have the capacity to feel anger, which is the Wood element. It is usually when there is an imbalance in that element that it draws particular attention to itself. If we are always angry or, alternatively, never angry then that concerns the Wood element

There are different schools of thought concerning this. One is that we each are of a different type of element intrinsically - some are Wood, some are Water for instance - and that this is the case since birth, determined not by our birthdate but by particular characteristics making that element the main focus for ourselves. Another school of thought is that all of the elements are expressed equally within us and that it is only when there is an imbalance in any one of them that they require specific attention. Continuing with Wood as an example, a lifetime of repressed anger may result in problems with the liver or with eyesight.

It is also pointed out by some practitioners that an element is only a 'window' through which we are permitted to see the unity behind - that there is, ultimately, only one element.

Whatever school is adhered to in Chinese healing, the means by which the elements are deduced remain the same. Observation of behaviour, sound of the voice, colour of the skin, food preferences, ailments and other clues give indication of the element or elements involved. These indications work in both extremes, whether the individual is strongly drawn to a certain factor or repelled by it - either way it means that there is an energetic 'charge' there.

To begin with, try the following experiment yourself:

Action

During the next twenty-four hours, every now and again, whenever you remember, listen to people's voices as they talk to you. Listen not so much to their words as to the sound of their voices. Ask yourself each time: What is that sound expressing? What are they really saying?

Often people use a lot of words to say something really simple. One person I knew in meetings would talk for ages about all sorts of issues, but the sound of his voice was expressing 'Listen to me! I'm confused and I want you to know that!'

In acupuncture the tone of the voice is often listened for. This is quite difficult, more difficult than simply listening to the tone to determine what is really being said, as in the exercise. Looking at the sounds in the table, for instance, it will be seen that that associated with the Earth element is 'singing'. Yet some languages have a distinct singing quality to them, such as Welsh. The 'moaning' sound associated with Water I often hear when a German is speaking English, though not when speaking their own language. Not only is it necessary to listen to what is 'behind the voice', sometimes you have to hear what is behind that too.

Radcliffe Camera, Oxford

Round shapes are of the Metal element and when on flat Earth are part of the Creative Cycle. This would also be true if surrounded by the Water element.

Other indications may be visual. A person always dressing in black clothes (or hating to wear black) may be enacting some dynamic relating to Water. An acupuncturist may look for a blue or black hue to the face.

Warning: Don't think that by understanding this concept, of symptoms indicating a 'charge' or 'energy' connected to a certain element, you can just make snap assessments of people, even of yourself. This method is notoriously difficult. One acupuncturist of ten years' experience told me that he and others of similar status could still make mistakes in identifying an individual's Constitutional Factor or CF. Even with ourselves this can be quite difficult as our capacity to fool ourselves is immense. The idea here is to give you an appreciation of the five elements and how they relate to individuals. Certainly you will have a much better idea of all this if you read the relevant books listed at the end of this chapter; and hopefully the case histories outlined here will gently nudge you in the right direction as well.

And 'gently' is the key word. Very little needs to be done, a recurring concept in this book. It is a greater awareness of every situation that we seek to encourage here and connected with that is the understanding that individuals are drawn to what they need at any particular time. For example, a chain-smoker may have a Metal imbalance - related to the lungs and to their breathing - but rather than attempt to stop them smoking, an understanding of what is behind their smoking may bring about a far easier termination to the habit.

As we are not in the way of 'intuitive acupuncture', the task is not so much to determine physical ailments but to develop a sensitivity to the elements involved, so it is a moot point whether a person is of one elemental 'type' or whether that emphasis changes. However, in Feng Shui one can become aware of how a process of healing is always underway, how people are attracted to particular elements at certain times in their lives. As one client was speaking to me, I thought, very faintly I could hear the sound of weeping in her voice - but it was far off, as if a lot of tears had been shed in the past but that things were now 'on the up'. She knew something of Feng Shui so I explained what I was picking up from her. She informed me that there had been a lot of tears in her life but that two years previously she had started a job in a circular building, which she knew now to be of the Metal element. "Somehow," she said, "working five days a week for two years in that place was a very healing experience."

The examples that follow will also sometimes demonstrate the nomadic, transitory nature of our experiences - and hopefully also convey a trust that we are drawn to what we need at particular times, an instinct that can be enhanced through greater understanding.

Wood

The element of Spring, of new growth. This is our ability to make plans, to sense a purpose to our lives by seeing ahead. When this ability is impaired we may become cynical, perhaps attempting to lose ourselves in drink, and lashing out angrily at those close to us. Or perhaps we cover our wounds with a false optimism, a naivety and reassurance that 'everything is all right'.

Anger is an important emotion. It can be like a thunderstorm clearing the air. When it is imbalanced it can either 'go missing' in that a person feels incapable of anger or it can become indulgent, a never-ending tirade, a 'dumping' on others. A Wood type of person may well become drawn to revolutionary social movements, anywhere where reform is needed. But if the source of the drive to change things is anger - anger at the world around, anger with one's own childhood - then the inner wound remains and no amount of outer change will heal that. A Wood person will always find another cause to fight for - a war may

end but not inside them. The 'Green' movement is a great vent for Wood issues, yet this too can result in extremes: the angry attack on a politician by the Greens in Germany in April 1999, resulting in missiles being thrown, is one example.

When there is energy around the Wood element, it is often provoked by issues from birth or childhood, the 'growing' stage. It is this that can give the impetus to change things in the world for the better - this can manifest in ecological issues, as stated, but also often in teaching or social welfare professions. When properly harnessed and in balance the potential for healthy and dramatic reform is immense, and the Wood type can give to others what they so often feel they themselves lacked in the past.

I came across one of the most painful situations relevant to this state of affairs when I was teaching a class of eight-year olds. I showed them a documentary about an 'island paradise' that had just been discovered off the coast of Canada, a place where dwarf black bears were friendly to humans as they didn't know otherwise. Stopping my enthusiastic monologue in its tracks, one of the children just looked at me and said, "It will be gone in ten years."

This is the world our children are growing up in.

Case Histories

Jason is a wood turner and sculptor by trade. Most of his life he has worked with wood and recently has dedicated himself to planting trees in Scotland and bringing attention to the ecological plight we find ourselves in. One of his striking sculptures is of four wooden skulls facing each other. The title of that piece is 'Conservation Conversation'.

When he talks there is a clipped tone in his voice and occasional outbursts of sarcasm.

Suspecting a Wood profile, I asked him:

"How do you envisage the planet's future?"

"There is no future," he replied. "I see devastation. Dead trees, a dead landscape. A holocaust."

"How do you feel about your birth and childhood?" I continued.

"That's the basis of my whole search," he said. "I did a lot of primal therapy years ago. I feel the whole key to my spirituality is in my growth issues."

In Jason's case, he was already quite aware of his issues around the Wood element and had spent a great deal of energy healing both what was inside and outside him. He was also quite emphatic that he saw our ecological sickness as an indicator of our spiritual malaise and that it was the latter he was mostly concerned with. "And basically," he said, "I see trees as being much better role models than politicians."

Talking about it was all that was needed to 'nudge' him further in that direction, though I also encouraged him to wear bright fiery clothes when in his workshop so that the next element in the creative sequence, Fire, was represented and that the Earth could be consequently nourished too - there was danger of it being controlled excessively by the Wood.

Sarah grew up with an alcoholic step-father who treated her extremely badly. For much of her life she involved herself with the feminist movement, therapy groups and ecological issues. She is a tall, muscular girl who wears thick glasses and dresses in green a lot. When she talks there is sometimes a sense of her being on the brink of rage. Despite this what really comes through is her compassion for others. She is a teacher and her compassion, combined with her strong organisational abilities, ensures that she is well-liked wherever she is. She gets things done - and with grace. Other suggestions of the Wood element are that she has a poor sense of direction, loves sour food such as saurkraut, dislikes windy weather and can't drink alcohol.

After I worked for her, she became passionately interested in Feng Shui for herself, eventually going on to study Permaculture (which effectively combines ecology with Feng Shui and many other disciplines). She also started seeing a therapist whose advice included many cushion-beating sessions in order to help her come to terms with her anger.

There was actually nothing that I needed to do as everything took care of itself and energy that could have become destructive instead became more pure in its compassionate and giving nature.

Fire

The element of Summer, of maximum flowering. Here is our ability to enjoy life to the full, to celebrate, dance and to laugh. When there is an imbalance we may become morose and sad or try and cover those feelings up by becoming The Clown - always making jokes, often at inappropriate moments.

The main organ associated with Fire is the Heart, but in Chinese medicine there is also the Heart Protector, more a function than an organ. While with child-like enthusiasm we may wish to be continually open to others, sharing our joys and our sorrows, the Heart Protector knows that that is not always wise, that boundaries need to be recognised - or we may end up becoming deeply hurt. When the Heart Protector is not functioning properly we might share our deepest concerns with strangers yet become cold and distant to those who love us.

'It is better to have lost in love than never to have loved at all' could be a phrase uttered by someone with a Fire profile. Love is a key issue for everyone but this is especially true around the Fire element, particularly the need to understand the different types of love. When boundaries have not been respected and a person has 'given their heart' inappropriately their emotions may cave in on themselves, resulting in a sullen introspection and the belief that 'it is better to have never loved at all'.

We all need love in our lives, particularly in our homes. In the past, fire was present in most of our houses. Now instead we often have the alien glare of the TV. This absence of real fire in our lives has partially been compensated for

through nuclear energy which acts as an imbalanced outlet of our need for fire, like a perverse variation on the real thing.

The magical pictures in the flames, the laughing and joking of friends around a bonfire or the romance of a dinner by candlelight... We receive much more than physical warmth from fire.

Case Histories

Marianne attended a workshop of mine in Spain. I was just starting to work with the different profiles of the elements and I introduced some of the 'clues' to the participants. Marianne and others knew immediately what her profile was.

She dressed in bright reds and oranges. She talked more than anyone else, effusively sharing all her joys and sorrows. (I saw her in the market a few days later doing the same with a stallholder she had never met before.) Her emotions fluctuated between high and low, sometimes within a few minutes. She could have us all laughing then would burst into tears, leaving everyone somewhat confused.

She told us that since the separation from her boyfriend of many years she had had many lovers, but hadn't wanted to commit herself to any. She also told us that she had always been aware of her volatile, fiery nature, which is why, since the separation, she chose to live by a river. "I always felt that I needed the water to control my fire," she explained.

At the time I lacked the experience to explore the issue further, but in hindsight - considering her lack of groundedness, her impractical nature and her proneness to fiery outbursts - instead of attempting to dowse her Fire, as she was doing, I would have preferred to channel it by introducing the next element of Earth. This could have been accomplished through many ways, including an emphasis on Earth colours in her home and perhaps an encouragement of 'earthy' activities such as cooking or gardening.

Perhaps, in time, such an outlet could have helped her broken heart to mend.

Simon leads quite a Bohemian lifestyle, never knowing where he'll be the following week. Commitment of any sort poses difficulties for him. His love life has always operated in extremes - deep, passionate and long-lasting affairs to numerous girlfriends to none at all. At first I suspected him to be of a predominantly Metal profile - there was a deep sadness in his voice, a suggestion of pain from his past, he smoked and he liked spicy foods. Then I realised that the sadness was not the lingering 'weeping tone' associated with Metal, but more the reactionary sadness from having been deeply hurt; and that his smoking indicated Fire rather than Metal because he smoked cigarillos, which he didn't inhale into his lungs, just enjoying their bitter taste. He also liked dark chocolate for its bitterness, drank coffee regularly and even deliberately burnt his toast sometimes. The spicy foods, it turned out, he could take or leave.

In his travels he often preferred hot countries, particularly desert terrain. It didn't matter too much if the heat were so extreme that nothing could be done.

Talking with him, it was clear that there were issues around his Heart Protector. Much of his pain had emerged from not being able to discriminate between his various types of relationships: all the women in his life, in particular, tended to blend into one. Consequently he would open up considerably to some he would never see again and close off to those who could possibly nourish him deeply. His openess to all and sundryr led to him being very popular and well-liked, one of the many strengths of those with a Fire profile, but inwardly he felt isolated and cut-off.

To build on the strengths of Fire, and to correct what imbalances he could, he undertook several tasks:

First, to simply be aware of the issue. This was encouraged by reading the relevant books and discussing things openly with those he felt he could trust.

Secondly, to act on his understanding. This involved visiting an acupuncturist and in daily life taking gentle risks with people, such as going to parties where he didn't know anyone.

Thirdly, to bring the Fire element more consciously into whatever environment he found himself in.

The latter was more difficult because of his lifestyle, but was accomplished in various ways. One was to often burn candles in his room, particularly one designed by a friend of mine to symbolise the Fire element - red, pyramidical with an aroma for the heart. Another method was to enhance the Fire position in his room. He preferred using the Black Hat method for the ba-gua, where Fire is in the middle of the wall opposite the door. By placing candles there along with bright reds, he felt it acting as a constant reminder that that was an area where healing was taking place for him.

Eventually, he found himself surrounded more and more by those with whom he felt a great degree of affinity. "The trick though," he informed me, "is to recognise my barriers and know exactly when to withdraw, to spend time by myself. In this way I can achieve the balance I always sought previously without knowing it."

For ultimately, he knew, he had to learn to love himself before he could love others.

Earth

Indian Summer is the time of gathering, before the arrival of Autumn. The Earth element in some of the old Chinese texts is also the last ten days of each of the four seasons - thus, all elements are gathered here. 'Everything that is created in the Universe meets at the centre and is absorbed by the Earth', states the Nei Ching ('The Yellow Emperor's Classic of Internal Medicine'). The Earth element

relates to our ability to nourish and be nourished. When this ability is impaired, we may have trouble giving or receiving. This can be physical - sometimes manifesting directly through eating disorders, particularly cravings for or aversions to sweet food - or mental, which is our ability to gather and process thoughts. When the latter is imbalanced we can lend ourselves to extreme worrying.

A person with an Earth profile often has a strong connection with their mother - their real mother, their maternal nature and/or their connection with Mother Earth. They can become 'Supermothers', always caring for others yet negligent of their own needs, or selfishly craving sympathy all the time, wanting somebody to mother them.

Concerns with the Earth element are paramount in this day and age, for obvious reasons. The highest percentage of resources per individual goes to America, which also has some of the worst undernourishment in terms of food 'goodness' - after all, the Americans are the inventors of junk food - while elsewhere citizens of Third World countries, with the highest populations, are dying of starvation. Yet every year mountains of food produce in the West are destroyed in order to maintain 'economic balance'. This is an eating disorder on a global scale.

In daily life the Earth element can manifest positively as the individual who does the cooking, feeds the family and visitors, and takes care of the home while everyone else sits around and talks about saving the world. Then, taking care of their own needs, that person can enjoy a delicious dessert, take off their shoes and socks and wander outside, bare feet in the long grass, and breathe in the air whilst looking up at the sky.

All the elements combined in a celebration of life.

Case Histories

Irmela is a homeopath and a mother. Much of her life seems to have involved taking care of others, which she loves to do. She is an excellent listener, which is an important factor in her success as a healer. When one talks to her the feeling she exudes is genuine sympathy and understanding.

At first the total absence of spices in the kitchen and the fact that she smoked a cigarette in her breaks - among other factors - alerted me to issues surrounding the Metal element, but eventually I saw that more as consequential from the preceding element of Earth. Whether that would be true from an acupuncturist's perspective, I had no idea, but the survey of Irmela and her house revealed a need to focus on Earth more than anything else. Other indications were that her front door was yellow - a colour she loved - and that her cookie jar was well-stocked! Overall though it was the quality of sympathy that was a deciding factor and the sense that she was better at taking care of others' needs than she was her own.

The two areas which I felt needed most attention were those which were primarily responsible for her nourishing herself: the kitchen and the bathroom, both in the Relationship/Marriage area of the house, also known as an Earth area in some systems.

From the Feng Shui angle, it was fairly straightforward. Both those key areas needed 'sprucing up'. This was accomplished largely in the kitchen by installing a new cooker. With the bathroom a quantum leap from it being functional to being luxurious was required. Bathrooms are often relegated to being merely functional in homes, yet they are where we go for transformation: to feel better. With that being the case, it should be done in style!

Jane is a very different case in that an imbalance around the Earth element can manifest through worrying. She can easily work herself up into a state about anything, turning molehills into mountains with the greatest of ease. When these concerns erupt, as they can quite frequently, she might even start crying until those around her feel obliged to offer her sympathy. Despite these outbursts she is generally extremely caring towards others and is well-thought of as a 'loving' person.

She also abhors sweet foods, preferring only to eat healthily, and her voice has a sing-song quality to it that is quite beautiful.

When she consulted me it was concerning issues of insecurity and also the state of mind she would frequently find herself in: she was worried about her worrying!

From my perspective, things were very simple: the central part of the house, known as Tai Chi and of the Earth element, was a corridor. That area connected to all the other parts of the house, including the upstairs, and was full of clutter: books, furniture, cleaning equipment and the children's toys. There was also a painting of a woman crying.

I got Jane to free that area up so that it would remain always near-empty and also to enhance it, painting the walls yellow and changing the picture for a more positive one. "Whatever happens in this area will affect what happens in the other areas," I explained.

One week after doing this, she enrolled in a computer training course, thus giving a healthy outlet for her mental activity, something she could focus on.

Metal

The element of Autumn, a time of preparation for the coming Winter. Here is our ability to enjoy the fruits of life, both physically through successful enterprise and spiritually through the gaining of wisdom. When this ability is impaired there is often a tendency towards innate sadness, a sense of something missing.

Feeling sad is an important quality in life, without which we can only ever be superficial, but when we do not grieve adequately we become stuck and feel unable to move on and get on with our lives. We become enshrouded in perpetual mourning. This can be for the loss of a loved one, whether through death or separation, or for the loss of 'golden' opportunities.

On a spiritual level this relates to coming to terms with our own deaths. Autumn is when nature 'dies' and, hence, at this time of year we are reminded of our mortality and questions start to arise, such as: Am I prepared for my own death, which can happen at any moment? When I die will I feel that I have really lived? Is my life rich in experience and wonder? Am I really making the most out of being alive?

Somebody whose experience in life is impoverished may try and make up for that lack through material wealth, but inwardly always feel empty. On the other hand, there could be a deliberate austerity, a denial of the richness of life by making poverty a virtue. Both point to issues surrounding the Metal element.

Intrinsic to both these extremes is the lack of a sense of self-worth. Someone with a Metal profile needs to feel valued, something they may seek by always being busy. They are consequently often very pragmatic which, when extreme, can manifest in a cynicism towards others' enthusiasm because they 'know better'. This arrogance can simply be a protection for they have a tendency to disassociate from their wounds and behave as if they're not there. The other extreme, as mentioned earlier, is to be perpetually enshrouded in grief, never moving on to new experiences. 'Everybody Hurts' could well be a theme song for the Metal types.

Physically, Metal relates to to the large intestine and to the lungs. The former is concerned with our ability to eliminate waste. Living in a room that is always such a mess it should be declared a national disaster area may be indicative of a Metal imbalance. A mess can be seen as symbolic of the past holding us back. (As a further warning about blindly following rules, I don't hold this to be true for every-one - teenagers' ch'i, for instance, can be so powerful they can live in any amount of disarray and remain perfectly healthy. Just don't go in their room too often.)

There is a connection with the lungs and the round shape of Metal in Feng Shui, for the the sky is perceived as being an upturned bowl containing stars - and air. This is true in Vaasta architecture sometimes as well, with the dome-shape being symbolic of the sky and of heaven and, when placed on a cuboid structure, shows God the Father and the Earth Goddess in perfect harmony.

Air pollution is a major issue in the modern world and in acupuncture the Metal element relates to our ability to take in the finer things in life - our sense of quality. When the very air we breathe doesn't measure up to that much-needed quality then both the physical and psychological implications are disturbing. When you take in a deep breath of fresh air, the vitality and well-being you experience demonstrate why Metal is connected with inspiration, for it represents our ability to absorb the sky - or heavenly ch'i.

Case Histories

David is a truck driver and mechanic. His proficiency in both these areas has earned him considerable respect from his peers. He often dresses in grey or grey-blue clothes. He once smoked at least ten cigarettes a day but then quit because of concerns for his health. There is a sadness at the back of his voice. He lost his father when he was very young and had to grow up very quickly, taking on many responsibilities when still a boy. He seems very aloof sometimes, cold and distant, which contrasts strongly with his affability and helpfulness towards others, especially when his comments border on the cynical.

A crucial aspect of those with the Metal profile is that they often cannot take in richness from the world around them, even compliments from others. This was reflected in David's work as a truck driver - hours, or days even, spent alone on the roads, cut off from friends and family, with only a small cabin as 'home'.

The first step was to enhance his work environment, to make it richer. This was accomplished through using strong scents in the cabin and varying the music and radio stations he would listen to. He started listening to audio books as well. (More about working with vehicles later in Chapter Eight.)

But the main step was actually taken by David directly through the interest he started to take in the Five Elements. Reading the literature, realising his connection with Metal, encouraged him towards further understanding of himself - and consequently healing.

When her husband died Madhu moved and then lived alone in a small house, all the walls of which she painted white. She smokes a lot. It is not just her voice that has a weeping tone to it, she exudes sadness as if she is continually on the verge of tears. Her food taste changed a lot over the years, she informed me - it is as if she wants her food to be as bland as possible, with no spices whatsoever.

Going around the house, it was the austerity of it that struck me. There was a lot of wood but the Metal-white walls controlled it so effectively that it didn't have a strong presence. Most of the windows faced West, the direction of Metal. As if all this weren't enough, there was a cemetery around the corner in near proximity to and visible from the house and a yin line (see Chapter Five) by the front road.

Part of the function of Metal is to allow us to experience grief and then move on. It was clear that Madhu had never got over the loss of her husband and was locked in perpetual mourning.

We talked about the situation and she cried a bit, saying that she realised she had put her life 'on hold' since her husband left her. She realised that she wanted to live her life fully again.

A move was imminent, she agreed. The house was associated with too much sadness for her. In the meantime, she would put glass-crystals in the windows to refract and soften the rays from the late afternoon sun and would consider bringing more colour into the rooms.

It was six months later that I heard from her. She told me she hadn't moved yet but that that was on the cards; also, that she had suddenly felt the urge to bring more colour into her life, it just felt right. She had painted the whole house except for one of the western rooms, which she left white in order to 'pay homage' to that direction and the lessons it had given her, particularly as regarded the value of our brief, fleeting lives - that every moment does, in fact, matter.

Water

The element of Winter, of withdrawal and introspection, and there is much about the Water element which concerns Mystery. It could be said that while Earth concerns our need for security, Water is about our need for insecurity. Those with a Water profile may seek danger, thriving on risk after risk; or they may be dominated by their fears, scared to go out of their house because of the unknown dangers that await. Those who watch horror movies incessantly are indicating a Water imbalance as are those who can't even hear mention of a ghost story without getting seriously frightened. In both cases the need to balance a need for Mystery, for the Beyond, is being expressed.

The ultimate mystery, most would agree, is Death - with its associations of sex and birth as well. We don't know where we come from nor where we go to. Faith can give a sense of security to the beyond but with so many differing 'structures'

for the spiritual life, when we add them all up together we are left with an unknowing as profound as when we began. Being comfortable as much as is appropriate with that unknowing is an important aspect of our lives which, when impaired, can result in morbidity or us becoming fearful or adrenalin-junkies; but when balanced may aid us in assessing risks accurately and responding with ease.

Courage, as has often been said, is not about being fearless but about being afraid to do something and doing it anyway. This clarity of purpose is one of the gifts of Water, associated with which is will-power or ambition.

On a scientific level also water is very much a mystery, its molecular qualities still not fully understood beyond the 'two hydrogens and one oxygen' that every schoolchild knows. It is also common knowledge that we ourselves are mostly water, as is the Earth - so much so that it has been suggested that the proper name for our planet is actually Ocean. The water we come into contact with though on a daily basis is unusual: 97 per cent of the planet's water is salty, 75 per cent of fresh water is polar ice and most of the remaining drinkable water is so deep underground as to be unreachable. The remaining fraction of a per cent i therefore extremely valuable, yet it is a commodity that is dwindling fast, with enormous repercussions on every level as we shall see in later chapters. Our sensitivity to this element is crucial if we are to survive as a species.

Our individual relationship with each element both physically and energetically is always worth looking at, as they are representative of each other. With Water, for instance, as well as attempting to assess a person's connection with the element generally, it is good to check their awareness of water itself in their environment. The presence of water through ponds or fountains may often be recommended in Feng Shui, but it is also important to know the quality of the water and from where it originates.

Case Histories

Elaine was a client who called me unexpectedly from a new flat. When I'd worked for her she lived in a small cottage, with no plans to move.

"I loved my cottage," she explained over the phone, "but after the Feng Shui I'd felt it had reached its optimum potential for me and I knew it was time to go. Now I want you to work on my new place."

On meeting her again, I found she'd changed. Before, she had given me the appearance of being a combination of fairly 'homely' and pragmatic, successful career-wise and content with her life; now she dressed entirely in black and seemed to have more of an edge.

The flat was an odd shape. None of the rooms were rectangular, but all with strangely-angled walls. Usually when the element of a place is so difficult to determine, it's because it's Water: irregular and unpredictable. (This is also true when a building seems to lack any coordinated planning, with extensions built all over chaotically.) And the feeling of the flat was watery, with no sense of 'fixture' anywhere within its four - or seven, or nine - walls.

Talking with Elaine, more became clear. Her cottage had been of the Earth element - solid, cuboid - and while it had given her the security she'd craved at the time, something enhanced through the Feng Shui, she'd come to crave more. The flat felt more 'right' for her at this stage in her life.

I realised that she was inviting more risk, more of the unknown, into her world. This was confirmed through further conversation and we then discussed the elements at play, with Elaine even more definite that this was the right place for her.

The only thing left to do in this regard was to give the flat some grounding. It was the lack of Earth that concerned me, for it is that element which defines Water, like a riverbank of clay or sea-stacks which so beautifully adorn some coastal areas. Too much Earth would dominate the Water through the control cycle, too little would allow it to disperse chaotically. In order to achieve the balance, we simply enhanced the central Tai Chi area of the flat, emphasising its Earth qualities through tan-coloured walls and the presence of weighty statues.

This did the trick, as Elaine informed me later, giving her still the sense of adventure she wished for but within acceptable parameters.

Tanya lives in a converted mill in a secluded river-valley. When she called me and gave me instructions over the phone how to reach her place, as the route was fairly complicated, I asked her at some point which direction the road was heading at a particular junction. "I don't know," she answered after some hesitation, "but I can inform you that the creek is flowing South at that point."

Tanya had spent many years living in a houseboat on the river nearby to the mill, and before that on other rivers. The mill had been derelict when she had been its neighbour and she had relied on the well in its grounds for a water-supply. Then news reached her that the mill was to be sold. This coincided with some money that came her way. Her initial move to buy the mill was simply out of concern that she would no longer have access to its grounds and well if she didn't purchase it. But gradually she began to renovate the building lovingly,taking care of it in a way it hadn't known for a long, long time. Her next step was to actually move in and start living on solid ground, quite a radical departure for her. This 'going with the flow' and ease of movement is characteristic of the Water element.

When we met, she was dressed mostly in blue. Her voice was slightly tremulous, but what may have once been a hint of trepidation in its sound now manifested as gentleness. She informed me that she was adopted as a child, with very little information about her parentage, though that changed later.

By this stage, the presence of the Water element had established itself quite firmly in my mind; it had also, I realised, established itself quite firmly in Tanya's life, but that this was very much a part of her that had balanced itself and now she was ready to move on.

The mill was gorgeous, she had done an impressive job. The large South-East window faced the river and an abundance of trees. Both Water and Wood were therefore well-represented. It was the next element, Fire, that seemed lacking and Tanya seemed ready for that element to be in her life. I encouraged her to bring in more green into the sitting room to 'echo' the forest, and to bring Fire highlights, through touches of red here and there, fiery cushions and the presence of candles in the evenings.

The next I heard she threw a party.

When I happened to visit a year later, it was late afternoon. We drank tea by the large window, through which could be heard the sound of birds and the river rushing by. Sunlight filtered through the leaves and bats frequently darted in and out, playing in the large eaves of the room. It felt like paradise.

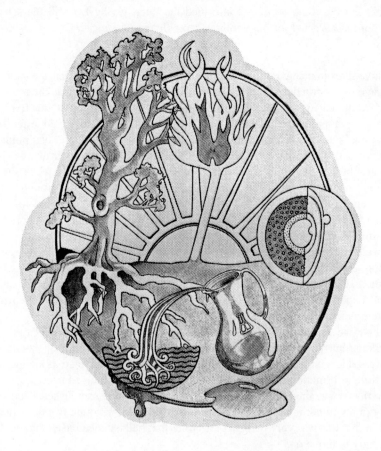

Jon Kane Houldsworth

Related Reading

Five Elements and Feng Shui:

Feng Shui Handbook	Lam Kam Chuen	(Gaia)
Feng Shui Handbook	Derek Walters	(Thorsons)
The Five Keys of Feng Shui	Sarah Bartlett	(Vista)
Interior Design With Feng Shui		
	Sarah Rossbach	(Rider)

Five Elements and Healing:

Dragon Rises, Red Bird Flies	Leon Hammer	(Station Hill)
Healing Your Emotions	Angela/John Hicks	(Thorsons)
Plant Spirit Medicine	Eliot Cowan	(SwanRaven)
Traditional Acupuncture: The Law of the Five Elements		
	Dianne M. Connelly	

Chapter 4

Lung Mei

Life is a bridge. Cross over it but don't build houses on it.

Indian saying

Crackle-Glazing

Lung mei are lines of concentrated ch'i in the earth, much like the bloodstream in the human body though a more correct analogy would be the meridians as used in acupuncture. The term 'lung mei' (pronounced 'loong my') actually means 'dragon veins' but is also popularly referred to sometimes as 'dragon paths' or 'dragon lines'. I tend to use the latter term as an overall one for all types of line, something many tend to do, as also with the colloquial 'ley line'. Some researchers get very pedantic about the use of certain words but I am not interested in semantic debates on this issue and will use popular terms quite happily, even using the vague designation 'line' on a frequent basis. What's in a name? (On occasion, though, I will have to be more specific.)

There is evidence of a connection between lines and other, cosmic influences, such as the rising of the sun on the 1st of May revealing the St Michael alignment in England, but the overall view is one of chaos, disarray, with harmony only operating at a deeper level. This fits with the fluidity associated with Taoism and early depictions of the lung mei in a landscape, as characterised by the popular 'crackle-glazing' in Chinese ceramics or the fault patterns in sedimentary rocks. What was perceived in the West as unaesthetic or 'faults' was understood to be beautiful in Taoism.

This difference in outlook persists today in various understandings of 'earth energies', with a preference in the West for the lines being straight conflicting with those who perceive them as meandering, like a river. There is less of a contradiction here than is apparent but before we find out why, a brief background sketch is necessary.

Patterns in the Landscape

There are parallel forms of understanding in other cultures: The Songlines of the Australian Aboriginals, Shamanic Lines of the Americas, Ceques in Peru, Fairy Lines of Ireland, Orang Bunian paths in Malaysia, the list goes on.

Geographic and cultural influences are obviously major factors in how the lines are perceived in various countries. How the 'lung mei' are perceived is derived largely from the Form School in Feng Shui, having been inspired by the spectacular mountain formations in Southern China where the Form School originated. Hence, a limitation becomes apparent by a tendency to associate dragon lines with outward forms, such as converging ridgeways known as a 'Dragon's Pulse'; for those outward forms may not always be available. Likewise, in Europe there is a reliance on ancient sites for the same reason, also revealing a restricting dependence.

To really be effective in determining the lung mei of a site you need to be able to go beyond forms. Australian Aboriginals, having very few if any outward markers in the outback, follow the turinga, using songs in order to delineate the various areas. No aboriginal can trespass onto another's songline unless he is given permission by being taught some of the song.

In the West an interest in 'leys' has emerged in the past century, giving rise to some complications and some controversy. The word 'ley' is derived from an old English word meaning 'clearing in a wood' and appears in numerous names, eg Chulmleigh, Botley, Ashleigh. The same is also true of the origin of the word 'hay' as in 'Roundhay' and if the clearing were created by a group rather than one individual the name could include 'ham' as in Nottingham.

Since Alfred Watkins in 1921 had his visionary experience of England being covered with a system of straight tracks, aligned by various neolithic and other ancient sites, some individuals in the West have been obsessed with discovering straight lines in the landscape. The dominant understanding in this field is that leys are straight. There are numerous magazines and books dedicated to this view with evidence to support it, though conventional archaeologists usually strongly refute it.

The reason for them being straight, some say, is that leys themselves are not natural. They have been created by people long ago in the past who knew how to harness and utilise the natural flow of earth energies. Standing stones and such like were erected for this purpose.

Another view is that the straightness of lines has nothing to do with 'energies' but that it indicates the 'path of the spirit' when it leaves the body.

Once again, I believe we can happily accommodate all these contradictions and even enjoy them, particularly by not getting lost in the various conflicting theories. It is much more practicable to concentrate simply on that which is useful to us - a key concept in this book.

Serpent Power

An indication of a way of resolving all these theories came to me seemingly by accident years ago.

I had just arrived on the island of Mallorca and, after a tiring journey, fell asleep in the afternoon only to wake up almost immediately from a strong dream.

My journey had taken me that day from Palma on the South coast along a hot dusty road via Inca and towards Alcudia in the North. In the dream I flew over the road, marvelling at how despite all the curves and meanders the road never actually changed its general direction.

In a flash, as I woke up, I realised I was looking at the ancient symbol of Caduceus: the meanders in the road were those of a snake entwined around a rod, Caduceus, of course, being the symbol of Mercury, the god of roads and communication.

This told me several things:

1. The rod was symbolic of what people referred to as 'leys'. A ley therefore was the average, the mean, of the undulating curves of the natural lines: a summary of their general direction.

Caduceus

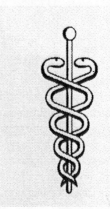

2. There are often two snakes in the Caduceus symbol. This implied that natural lines - which I shall refer to as dragon lines or simply 'lines' from now on - sometimes worked in pairs. This was very possibly indicative of a yin/yang pairing. Hamish Miller's work on the St Michael and St Mary lines (and later on the Apollo and Athena lines) would seem to support that.

3. It would follow that the node points - where the two snakes crossed - would be where the energies were balanced, particularly maybe at the base point where they originated - if they had an origin. Healing - another association with Caduceus - would involve bringing the two energies harmoniously together.

4. Old roads and tracks sometimes followed the 'average' direction of lines, thus confusing the perception of those who understood the roads and lines to be synonymous. They weren't synonymous but roads once had a tendency to follow the natural flow of ch'i;

something sadly missing in modern road-building; for the experience of travelling along a line can put one in touch with the subtle forces of the Earth as we shall see in the final chapter. I should acknowledge here that Watkins never actually thought of a ley as having anything to do with 'energy', only with an alignment of sacred sites. There are many who would agree with him today while others distinguish between a ley and an 'energy ley', a six to eight foot wide straight beam of yang energy.

Tracing a Line

There are many ways of detecting a line and the books listed at the end of this chapter give valuable advice on how to do so but it is necessary to give a rough outline here before we proceed to some more complex takes on the situation.

Road aligned with Brent Tor, Dartmoor

Old paths - Old trackways often followed the natural flow in the earth.

Roads - Roads are often built on older ones which, in turn, were built on old tracks. In Europe blacksmiths' cottages are sometimes indicative of this.

Nature - The fauna and flora on a line are often very abundant. This is because of the concentration of ch'i.

Atmosphere - The ambience of a place is often one of the best indications. Important places on a line usually have quite a telling atmosphere, hopefully an extremely strong sense of well-being but, if the line is unhealthy, the sense will be of malaise - even, perhaps, horror.

People - Individuals are usually affected very strongly if living on a major line. A friend told me once of how a psychiatrist was doing open sessions one day in England and virtually every person who turned up (independently of each other) were from the same village. I checked my map of the area and found an unhealthy line going right through the village, one I had been studying for some time. Conversely, healthy lines often keep close friends together even when miles apart. I often get clients who know each other well and are living in close proximity to the same line, though not to each other.

Churches and shrines - Modern religions often built their places of worship on older, sacred sites. This was in order to persuade the followers of the old religion to keep visiting the same place, albeit under a new name. You can often find ancient pagan symbols in English churches, such as the 'Green Man' spewing vegetation out of his mouth. Names often just took a slight change. 'Black Annis', an aspect of the dark matriarchal goddess, could become 'St. Anne', for example. Sometimes this would happen deliberately, sometimes accidentally. Similar patterns will be found in other parts of the world with different religions.

Maps - A detailed map is one of the best tools you can use. With it you can spot some alignments straight away and draw them on the map. This will have to be confirmed by actual field work though.

Dowsing - Dowsing is a skill that most people have and very few actually develop. To learn this skill properly you need to spend a lot of time practising, reading up about it and preferably learning from somebody who is already well-experienced in this. Dowsing is only essential in order to establish the exact position of a line, even if that line's influence extends far beyond its actual dimensions.

Even experienced dowsers can disagree as to the location of lines, thus giving fuel to their detractors, yet agreement can also be reached even without the individual dowsers meeting or exchanging notes. Inexperience can play a big role in contradictory results but there is a tendency also for different dowsers to 'tune in' to very different things - some people are very good at finding water, others geopathic stress lines for instance. Finally, as a line's influence can be quite extensive some dowsers respond to particular frequencies of its energy that are complicated further by the presence of yet even more lines.

Once again the trick is to focus and discern what is actually relevant.

Above all the tracing of a line usually depends on two things:

1. **Observation.**
    Using maps and fieldwork the trick is to discern patterns, a repetition of certain themes moving in an approximately unified direction across the land.
2. **Intuition.**
    Often the most direct method, there is no way to teach this except to encourage openness and receptivity, a trusting of one's instincts. Clues may come, for instance, through particular songs entering your head at particular places.

You may recognise these two qualities as emanating from the left and right sides of the brain, which they are. The logical and intuitive sides of yourself need to work together - the crystal and the dragon.

Summary of Clues for the Presence of a Line:

Old paths and roads
Specific directions followed by wildlife
Ancient sacred sites
Abundant nature
Strong atmosphere
Similar behaviour patterns of people
Association with particular songs at the same place
Names of places eg Chorley
Observable alignments eg churches in a straight line
Your intuition

But don't jump to conclusions! Tread carefully.

A Ball of String

Take many pieces of different-coloured string, scrunch them up into a ball and throw them on the ground. There in front of you is a fairly accurate depiction of earth energies on a site.

For no matter how skilled and sensitive you become in detecting energy lines you are likely to be confused at first by the sheer amount of information you are receiving. Again, it is a question of discernment. The modern mind tends to have much more difficulty with simplicity than it does with complexity: it prefers things to be as elaborate as possible.

There is a story that one day in discourse Buddha held up a tangled ball of string. "How do you untangle this?" he asked his disciples. Theories and different ideas were put forth but Buddha said nothing. Eventually, after a long period of silence, one disciple stood and walked up to Buddha. He held out his hand and asked for the string. Buddha gave it to him. The disciple looked closely at the string then untangled it. Buddha smiled.

Nowadays all the disciples who had theories about the ball of string would have obtained university degrees.

Using the techniques listed in the previous section to discover a line you will have focused on one 'piece of string'. This is actually all you need to do at first, for usually you will have intuitively found the most influential line on a site, perhaps with one or two secondary influences.

The latter can be of many types. Not only do we have the main 'arteries' affecting a site, we also have minor lines - 'capillaries' - leys, fault lines, underground water and lines from electromagnetic sources such as microwave towers. For a detailed analysis of a site a dowser will actually map out all of these and more.

In the meantime, though, we are concerned here only with the mainline 'arteries' and it is these which usually provoke most interest.

It will be noted that visual examples accompanying the text depict lines that are straight rather than meandering. This is purely for convenience. Dowsing will reveal the details of curves and departures from the line's direction but this is not necessary to determine the line's character. In short, what we have here is the 'rod' of the Caduceus. It is also not necessary at this stage to complicate issues with 'companion lines' - one will be easily enough to get on with, though we will finish this chapter with an example of lines working in parallel.

The Influence of Lines

Common questions asked are, "How wide is a line?", "How long is a line?" and "Is it good to live on one?".

There are no easy answers to any of these and, naturally, dowsers and researchers tend to disagree. You will have to find out for yourself but, for what it's worth, I shall answer from my own (and others') experience:

The Width

Actually dowsing a line often reveals its width to be less than a metre, with the smaller 'capillary' lines being less than a tenth of a metre, but the influence can extend so far that it tends to be merely of pedantic interest where the actual line is. The line can be likened to an electric wire, with the extent of its electromagnetic field being what really interests us. The only time we really need to accurately map the line's course is to determine if it goes through a particular site or not; and when we wish to work with it directly, about which more later.

The Length

The length of a line varies considerably. Smaller lines are less than a kilometre in length, while some researchers claim evidence of bigger lines circumnavigating the globe. The situation is even more complex in that lines have a tendency to 'harmonise' with each other, as we shall see in the next section, and to lose distinction. Usually when people talk about a 'ley' they mean a line a few kilometres in length, perhaps beginning and ending at key points, such as ancient wells. This tends to be more of academic interest than anything else, the best way to learn being to investigate a site and discern the various influences for yourself.

Is it good to live on a line?

As to whether it is good to live on a line, that depends. The major lines are usually too powerful for dwellings, with inhabitants besieged by various forces which they usually don't understand. An old Irish method for ensuring that this didn't happen was to place a stick at each of the four corners of a proposed site, leave them overnight then return in the morning to check: if any of the sticks had 'fallen' over in the night then that meant there was a fairy path there and they shouldn't build in that place. There are bound to be subsidiary lines through a house, though, and they can be of benefit, bringing the much-needed ch'i inside at a more manageable level.

The main question to ask, regarding whether it is benign or not to live on a line, is: Can you handle it? For the energy that comes into your house demands a specific way of living that will be unique to that line. Even churches and cathedrals, built on old sacred sites where many lines converge, only really flourish if they 'give voice' to the specific energies on that spot. For example a place of dominant yin energy would 'prefer' a church dedicated to St Mary or another female saint.

A very dramatic example of disharmony with the environment on an energetic level concerns a phenomenon that we will return to eventually: Two churches in Suffolk, England, experienced on the same day in the sixteenth century a sudden thunderstorm with apparitions of huge black dogs appearing at the altars. Two parishioners kneeling and praying were struck dead in one church. Only by labelling the apparitions as 'hounds of hell' were people at all comfortable with these events, yet the black dog is common in folklore in many countries and the pagan sites on which the churches were built almost certainly had more sympathy towards the phenomenon.

In ancient China the one type of building likely to be found in close proximity to a dragon line would be a pagoda, its shape being considered harmonious with the earth current, both stimulating it and being stimulated itself. The average secular dwelling, though, would not be placed by a main line, but will be nestled amongst the smaller 'capillaries'. This is a wisdom followed by other cultures as well, till fairly recently. Aerial infra-red photography reveals that houses in Regensburg, Germany, were built until the mid-nineteenth century always next to underground streams but never crossing them - streams, of course, being indicative of a flow of ch'i via the lines. Nowadays people build wherever they want and at some cost to the environment and to themselves,

In summary, to answer the question 'Is it good to live on a line?' we return to the related question: 'Can you can handle it?' In Ireland, if a house were inadvertently built on a fairy path, the occupants would have to keep doors or windows in alignment with the path open at night to 'allow passage', which is one way of dealing with it. This, like other solutions, is merely remedial though and generally one would advise against building on a line.

As to whether it is wise to build in close proximity, the answer will vary according to individuals and to individual lines. Even extremely unhealthy lines can be 'tempered' at specific points by the influence of other, more benign, lines meeting them at an angle.

We will be looking at all of these aspects in some depth.

A Line Example

Look at the accompanying map of Oxford. The two lines drawn in have been discovered by previous researchers. Numerous clues attest to their existence, such as the churches in alignment, so beloved of 'ley' researchers. Also, the horizontal line runs adjacent to Botley Road towards the West of the city.

Sketch Map of Oxford

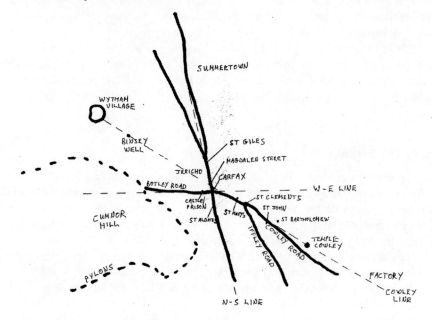

Showing main roads and alignments. Taken from the author's field notes.

Here the clues are external and deduced from objective reasoning but the questions I would ask require a more subjective approach as well - one of feeling.

For example:
The two lines meet at the centre of the city at a crossroads known as Carfax. This is known to Oxford residents as a place prone to considerable traffic congestion. How does that feel to you? How do you think it might affect the lines?

Historical research reveals that Oxford used to receive its water from the natural springs in Cumnor Hill at the far end of Botley Road. The water was then pumped to Carfax. Nowadays the water is from an artificial reservoir a few miles North of Cumnor Hill. Does this strike you as an improvement or a turn for the worse?

Visitors to the city have expressed to me their surprise at arriving in the centre to find 'nothing there'. Nothing that is except for shops and traffic. What does that indicate?

Botley Road itself suffers from considerable congestion. It is also underneath electricity pylons. Even without launching into research of the effects of electromagnetic fields, what is your instinctive reaction to all of this?

Next to the Norman Castle on the line is a prison, no longer used. Could this have had an influence on the line?

These are just a few of the questions that would be appropriate in such a case. Further questions arise, such as: if ch'i from the traffic and electricity is exacerbating the situation, what are the alternatives? Can something be done to improve matters at Carfax?

This is where the lung mei have obvious environmental implications and where we cross in one leap from something that seems mostly of esoteric or insubstantial relevance to something that has an obvious and direct impact on where we live. Town planners take note.

Lizard's Back

The previous example gives indications of determining just how healthy or not a line is, something affected considerably by human activity. Determining this is key to working with the lung mei and we will be looking in the next chapter at going further in this regard, with advice on how to work practically with the lines. Before that, let's take a jump into the deep end.

The methods to use in order to establish the actual nature of a line are the subject of the next chapter so if descriptive terms such as 'healthy', 'watery' etc. seem confusing, be patient. All - or, at least, quite a lot - will be revealed.

After having read this far and studied the accompanying examples of lines you should by now have grasped some of the basic characteristics and know, at least

Lizard's Back, Cornwall

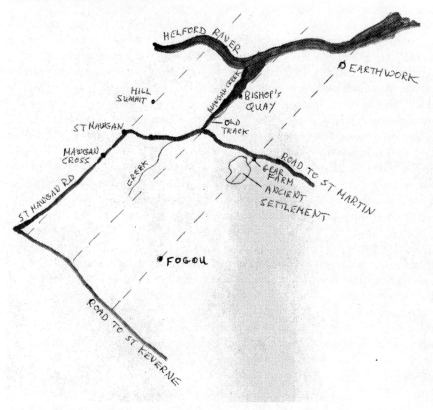

Sketch reproduced from the author's field notes.

in part, what to look for. Complexities start to arise when you survey a site as a whole, but even then simplicity is the key. The example accompanying this page is an area by Helford River in Cornwall, England. It is an interesting case history from many perspectives.

As already stated, Britain is one of those countries fortunate with their preservation of the past. In this example, my client lived near Mawgan village and was surrounded by many artefacts such as ancient stone crosses, old churches, standing stones etc - all obvious indications of the directions in which earth energies could be moving.

There are a number of lines moving on a North-East/South-West axis. If you move from the stone cross in Mawgan and go to the church and continue you will be following one of the lines. Another goes from the fogou (an ancient chamber in the earth) nearby to Gear Farm then further towards an earthwork; another is manifest partly as an old farm track a bit further along the road - and higher - between the mill and Gear Farm, following the river towards Bishop's Quay.

These three lines and possibly others are moving in unison, forming what I call a 'Lizard's Back', leading to and over Helford River. In classical Feng Shui when ch'i follows a ridgeway it is called 'Dragon Veins' and if the ridgeway is extremely prominent it is called a 'Dragon's Backbones'. When I first discovered the pattern of numerous lines moving in near-parallel courses I called the formation a 'Lizard's Back', having been inspired by Australian Aboriginal paintings depicting the parallel lines of 'ridges' on a lizard, though the lines do not necessarily always follow ridgeways. The name fits particularly well in this case in that this is an area of Cornwall known as 'The Lizard'.

There are other lines - and other ridgeways - evident in this case, but I find that the Lizard's Back formation is so powerful, with each of the parallel lines in harmony with its companions, that it tends to take precedence over the general influence of other lines and usually in a very fortuitous way.

Part of the power of the Lizard's Back must be in the way the lines support each other. Here they are mostly in excellent health - you'll have to take my word for it as I'm the one who got my boots dirty - particularly the Mawgan line which is very yin, feminine, and supported by the tributes, at the time I went, to Princess Diana in the church. It is very unusual to find a yin line in such good health, as we shall find out, though perhaps not in Cornwall which retains much of its past, matriarchal heritage. The Gear Farm line is more yang and not quite so happy (at the time of investigation) but even that is healing, encouraged by its companions. The Bishop's Quay line is - appropriately - watery and cool, following the course of Mawgan Creek.

With this example it should be apparent that any academic questions - such as 'Where does a line begin and end?' - become less than useless because we are focusing on one particular area and wish to understand the nature of that area.

A further complication could have arisen here if strong lines with very different energies had come from other directions. This wasn't the case here and, as I said, the Lizard's Back has a power to be respected. My client's house was suitably nestled between these lines and others nearby, without being on top of any of them: an ideal site as regards the lung mei.

Related Reading

The Dance of the Dragon	Hamish Miller/Paul Broadhurst	(Pendragon)
Fogou	Jo May	(Gothic Image)
The New Ley Hunter's Guide		
	Paul Devereux	(Gothic Image)
New View Over Atlantis	John Michell	(Thames and Hudson)
The Old Straight Track	Alfred Watkins	(Methuen and Co.)
The Sun and the Serpent	Hamish Miller/Paul Broadhurst	(Pendragon)

Chapter 5

Stalking the Dragon

Man follows the earth.
Earth follows heaven.
Heaven follows the Tao.
Tao follows what is natural.

- Lao Tzu

Individuality of Lines

Crucial to the methods outlined in this book for working with the lung mei is developing an appreciation of the individual nature of each line you examine. There are many ways to seek an understanding of the nature of a line and you are likely to develop your own methods, but here are some guidelines:

The first thing to note is that any line will have a constant theme to it, no matter how far you move along it. This theme will vary in its expression but its essence will not. You can think of it as a long piece of rope where the colours change periodically along it but it's always the same rope. Or think of it as a song which changes its rhythm or incorporates various tunes at different times - but it still remains the same song.

One way to determine what the main theme is is through observation. Once you have reason to suspect the presence of a line, attempt to plot its approximate course on a map. Then look at the places on the map which the line crosses. Do any historical research that is necessary. Unsubstantiated stories are important as well, for myths are the language of the unconscious and folklore can be extremely useful in this regard. In other words, treat everything as being of possible symbolic significance.

The intuitive aspect of this is likely to manifest through feelings, gut-instincts, songs popping into your head whenever you're in a particular area, dreams may come to you at night about certain places on a line. As the more intuitive among us tend to say, "I don't know how I know, I just know."

Unfortunately the latter statement can sometimes result in an imposition of one person's 'feelings' onto another. Similarly, the analytical approach of drawing lines between important landmarks can also be insisted upon by its followers of being 'right'. This is why when doing this work it is always important to be aware of how little one knows.

Follow a line, get to know it, but be like those mentioned by Lao Tzu: 'Watchful, like men crossing a winter stream'.

Dragons, Tigers - and Kookaburras

With Feng Shui I actually distinguish between 'dragon' and 'tiger' lines, the former being yang and the latter yin. A semantic complication arises here though as the lines themselves are seen as active yang energy in the passive yin earth. This is expressed by yang, celestial ch'i meeting the yin, passive earth (eg in the form of rain) and enlivening it, producing raised places such as a ridgeway.

To add to the confusion, as we look in more detail at different types of lines, we will see that there are more variations on these themes. For example, some yin lines are simply 'female' in their character, while others are 'death' lines suitable only for burial grounds.

It is therefore important to approach the subject with a certain degree of freshness and not get caught in historical traps. This will enable us to learn from the past and not get stuck in it. Keeping this in mind it is possible to untilise concepts such as yin and yang, treating each line individually without attempting to mould it into conceptualism. One example of the adaptability needed as regards symbols and names is a case I had in South-West Australia.

The house I was asked to look at had a long history of severe problems with the inhabitants. No matter how they started when they moved in, things would turn for the worst almost immediately, often leading to violence. The house had changed hands many times.

Before I actually got to the place I had an uncomfortable feeling about the assign-ment. I had had previous experience with going in too deep when extremely negative earth energies were involved and the toll they would have on anyone physically and emotionally was not to be underestimated. My intuition seemed to be warning me yet, with my customary insatiable curiosity, I forged ahead.

On arriving, I couldn't actually go onto the grounds because of the delicate situation - I was acting on behalf of the landlord, not the inhabitants - but I stopped on the road by the driveway. The sign to the house was dilapidated with several letters missing. It was a hot, still day and through the heat haze I could see the wooden house, alone in that barren area, with an oppressiveness surrounding it that was virtually tangible.

Almost immediately the problem was apparent. There was an unhealthy line adjacent to the driveway, as dowsing confirmed. I looked at some hills to the North, because that is where I sensed the unhealthy flow coming from, but I could see nothing obvious.

The line almost certainly lay on the edge of the house if it didn't actually go right through it. I knelt down, in order to absorb the energy more, all the time warning bells going off in my head.

Suddenly I heard a laugh. I looked up and saw, above the line on a dead, twisted tree was a kookaburra. My impression was that it was laughing at me.

I took it as a warning and left.

Later that day I discovered two things. The first was that the hills I had been looking at were where extensive mining was taking place. The mining was controversial and farmers in that area had a tendency to get badly sick, seemingly without cause.

The second thing I discovered was an aboriginal legend about a man who dared to go into a particularly dangerous area of the dreamtime. As he stepped into the dreamtime he heard a kookaburra laughing at his foolishness. Taking no heed, he forged ahead to dire circumstances.

It's not surprising I was being laughed at for I was clearly out of my depth, there was nothing I could do about the source of the problem and no good would have come out of my interference.

Going With The Flow

In the above example I mention the 'flow' as coming from a particular direction. This is my - and others' - experience that it does so, but it can only be determined by dowsing and/or intuition. Hence, there is plenty of room for disagreement. My advice, as usual, is to find out what works for you and to stick with that for as long as it is useful.

One way in which 'the flow' of ch'i is relevant is if you follow the line. This is one of the most efficient ways of understanding the lung mei. An ancient Chinese description of a 'dragon man' at work shows him sitting quietly on a rock, then suddenly getting up and running in a particular direction, stopping and walking back to the rock, then repeating the whole performance several times but in various directions. He was following the flow of ch'i.

I personally am too lazy to run but I'm quite happy to walk the length of a line if it takes no more than half a day or so and to do that I try and first determine the direction the ch'i flows in. This is not necessarily that important, because you will meet the same things whichever direction you move in, but I have found that people tend to have a clear sense of what direction a line is moving in and often prefer to keep with that direction.

Whichever direction you follow, if the distance is great and time is limited you can also drive along the line.

On your journey along a line, however you are travelling, pay attention to any symbols. Remember that you are seeking a pattern. Observe the wildlife. If you see a fox running along the line, for instance, ask yourself what that might mean. Perhaps Native American or Celtic associations with particular animals may help, but tread lightly. Don't get restricted by ideas of symbols, for you are working much deeper than that - through direct experience.

I personally use symbols quite often to give names to lines, simply for convenience. The Australian example, naturally, I always thought of as the

'Kookaburra Line' in the future, though if I had continued the research into the hills I may eventually have come up with something else. Sometimes the name emerges from a road the line moves along, sometimes simply from a particular feeling. When working with groups of people on the lung mei of an area I find there is almost always unanimous agreement in the name to use - in fact, the name usually just 'happens' without any conscious decision being made at all.

Hands On Earth

By now more questions have probably arisen for you, having read this far, of which one must be about the 'hands on the earth' approach I used for the Kookaburra Line. I find this one of the most direct and efficient methods for assessing a line's qualities. Bodyworkers are often very good at this, noticing the similarities between the Earth and the human body. This is how you do it:

Action

Once you have estimated the whereabouts of a line you need to be able to find its centre, its core, though dowsing and/or intuition. At this stage it is necessary to be that accurate.

When you have found a point directly on the line, kneel down and put your hand or hands on the earth at that place.

Close your eyes.

Note anything that could be important: What do you feel? What thoughts are passing through your mind? What symbols? What do you notice in the ambience around you? Think: If the line were a colour or colours what would it/they be? If it were sound what kind of sound?

Experiment with this anywhere you like. It doesn't necessarily have to be on a major line; if you try looking for a line even in your garden or house you will find one, albeit most probably a smaller 'capillary' but that will do just as well.

Here we come to an absolutely vital point of working with a line's ch'i:
Once you have explored a line sufficiently you will have a good sense and understanding of what its nature is.

The next stage is to: *Establish to what extent the situation above the line is expressing that nature.*

This is the most important concept to grasp about working with the lung mei in this chapter. Testimony to the destructiveness of mankind NOT living in harmony with the lines is global. To illustrate this point I am about to give a number of case histories. Before that, another important subject needs to be mentioned first.

Horse riding provides a happy medium between walking and driving and bridleways are often echoes of ancient tracks, following the 'ley' of the land.

Black Streams

When a person is wounded, whether physically or emotionally, they tend to withdraw from others. If this is for a short period then it is just a brief reaction, for example after having been insulted; but if the withdrawal - perhaps after ongoing abuse - is long lasting, without any signs of a healing occurring, then the situation has become a problem.

This holds true for the Earth as well. An area that is healthy will have an abundance of ch'i near the surface, expressed in the well-being of plants, animals and people.

A place that is hurt withdraws its ch'i. In such a case the task of the Feng Shui practitioner, whether working on the interior design of the house or the earth energies of the site, is to encourage the ch'i back.

'Black stream' was a term used by dowsers when they first came across unhealthy lines and assumed, erroneously, that they were always connected with underground polluted water. The truth is that sometimes there is a connection, sometimes there isn't.

Remembering that a dragon line is a concentration of ch'i, one expects a place with that line to be abundant with energy. A black stream is when the line has been badly hurt, usually through long-term abuse, and the ch'i withdraws, leaving a ghastly emptiness in its place. Physically this can manifest through accidents, decay, destruction, dilapidation, pollution, sickness; on an emotional level a sense of depression is felt, hopelessness, an intangible knowing that something is wrong. This will persist right along the line, usually for miles, with variations on the theme being in evidence beginning to end.

Black streams are now very common, so a word of warning here:

When you work directly with earth energies you are very vulnerable. This is because you are opening your senses to an extent that most people never do. This increase in sensitivity means that you absorb ch'i - both healthy and unhealthy - to an enormous extent, usually in a very short time. This is why many practitioners working on this level take steps both to protect during and to cleanse themselves after a survey.

At the beginning of my research into black streams I was wary of one such line on the edge of Dartmoor. When a fellow science teacher was planning a day's journey to the moor, I realised he would be 'cruising' the line for a few miles but I said nothing for he had till then displayed strong prejudice against my new-found interest. He had an accident at the very spot I'd marked on my map as the most dangerous. Fortunately he was not hurt except emotionally and later admitted to me that he had 'felt weird' in that area and 'was there a funny energy there?'.

When working directly on a line, whether touching and absorbing its energy or 'stalking' it, if that line is a black stream, then protection is essential.

How this is done is a personal choice. I often carry particular gemstones for protection - such as black tourmaline and moss agate - while others use aura soma or simply meditation methods. Afterwards, if the survey were a demanding one, I usually avoid speaking to anyone more than necessary, taking time to have a shower, to rest and recuperate. Bodyworkers such as masseurs or rebalancers often take similar precautions so none of this is unusual.

In a nutshell: be careful.

In addition, it must be mentioned that one of the basic procedures adhered to by most dowsers is to *ask permission* from a line or place before working on it. You can do this by asking it in your mind or by using a pendulum. This precaution shows respect for the location and precludes any possibility of you going where you're not wanted: if you hear 'No' then it's best to retreat until the time is right, if it ever will be. In the next chapter I will give an example of what happens 'when fools rush in', namely me.

Ways To Protect Oneself

- Carry protective stones
  eg Black tourmaline, moss agate, malachite, sugalite
- Carry a protective symbol
  eg The Om, the Cross
- Use a Tibetan prayer wheel which, when turned clockwise, boosts
  the etheric body (cf Chapter 7)
- Imagine yourself surrounded with white light
- Use strengthening scents from aura soma or aromatherapy
- Don't work alone - be with those you trust
- Avoid spending too long in difficult areas
- Have a good laugh, enjoy yourself
- Smoke a cigar (my own favourite Native American technique)
- After a survey, take a shower and time to come back to yourself

Death Line

I had given a two hour talk one evening on - among other things - the effects
of living in the proximity of an adverse line. After the talk, a woman approached
me to say she was startled to hear my list of problems associated with such a line,
such as nausea, depression, inexplicable accidents etc. She told me she worked in
the town's university and there was one building that had an immense number of
such problems with the inhabitants though no-one could tell why. "I can't walk
down the corridor there without wanting to vomit," she told me. "Every director
who arrives healthy and enthusiastic becomes sick and depressed within two
years..."

An architect who attended the talk overheard this and came over to join us.

"The university is by the hospital, isn't it?" he asked.

"Yes," she said. "Why?"

"Well, you know what they say about the hospital: 'If you go in, you don't come
out again.'"

I found out later that this was true - it did have that reputation - but that also,
paradoxically, the hospital had been known to deal with very demanding
near-death cases successfully.

It will be apparent at this stage in the story why I am not naming the place -
there's enough controversy already about this sort of work without having to deal
with angry ambassadors. Suffice to say this took place in quite a hot country.

I met with the lady again, when she brought a map of the town. I looked at
where the university building and the hospital were. The size of these buildings
made accuracy difficult but it was possible to imagine them on a line

which extended further South-West - to a few points on an approximately straight course.

"What are these places?" I asked, pointing at two of them as I didn't understand the language.

"They are cemeteries," she informed me, "one Jewish, the other Christian."

This was interesting. If these were old burial grounds it was possible we were dealing with a very yin line, perhaps a sick one - a black stream, as my friend suspected.

I noticed another point on the same course. "What is this?" I asked.

She looked at me with wide eyes. "That is a chapel," she said. "A chapel built entirely out of human bone."

Some time later I decided to visit this town and to actually stalk the line in order to get to know it better. If it really were as bad as she thought, I would just terminate the experiment and leave the line.

I began by the river and walked North-East, using a compass and intuition to guide me, but also knowing some of the places I had to visit on the way - all of which were cemeteries. Almost immediately I met a funeral procession. The subjective feeling I also received fairly promptly was a strange one: it was of my imminent demise. I felt death no longer as a vague happening in my future: the reality of it was in the present. I could die at any moment. Surprisingly this didn't feel disturbing - for it was simply the truth, albeit a truth we mostly tend to ignore as much as possible. As I walked on I felt I understood for the first time the Mexican Dia del Muerte - the Day of the Dead, celebrated with festivities and candy-skulls.

I passed the many graveyards, stopping only to marvel at the bone-chapel with its hundreds of skulls staring out from the inner walls. The monks were not being morbid when they built it - they had simply and probably instinctively understood the nature of the site as a place to confront death rather than evade it.

Further research showed that most of the buildings suffering from the line were built in the twentieth century. Although no-one asked me to work on the hospital or university, I later had a client who lived in a block of flats adjacent to one of the cemeteries. I had to make it clear that there was nothing unhealthy about the line at all - it was performing its function perfectly as it always had done. But it was totally inappropriate to build living quarters on top of it. Using it for prayer, meditation or burial was fine - anything else not. Living on top of such a line can instill such extreme pressures on the psyche that few are likely to put up with them easily. In most cases it is best to move. In the case of my client, once she was aware of the full picture, she decided to take protective measures and to use the energy to meditate. If that proved too difficult in the long term, then she would move, she informed me. As for the person in the university, she dealt with it by limiting her time in the building considerably and always carrying protective gemstones.

Active Line

Once again I have to avoid possible upset by not naming the place where this little story took place, except that we are now in northern England. Fortunately we don't need a map to illustrate the point.

I received a call from a couple who refused to be specific on the phone about what the nature of the problem was, only that they had one and that it involved people around them.

On the day of the appointment I arrived early, as I usually do, in order to spend time in the surroundings. I had already consulted a map so I knew what I wanted to check out.

My clients lived on a hill. The road leading to their house (one of many terraced houses) led straight up the hill, also on which was a road junction and a cemetery. It was the latter I wanted to explore.

It was a very large cemetery that sprawled a good way up the hill. It was also very light and airy, with few shady spots. A study of the stones told me something else: the earliest stones were late nineteenth century, a time by which our instinctive 'sense of place' had become sadly diminished. This was not an old site.

The little chapel had red signs daubed onto its walls, mostly satanic symbolism, but that was only symptomatic of where the real problem lay.

The height, the atmosphere, the openness of the site made the cemetery extremely yang. For burial purposes you need the earth ch'i to be yin enough to 'absorb' and regenerate the ch'i of the once-living in such a way that it is available for the earth once more. A yang site won't regenerate anything but, instead, will keep the ch'i active. This quality was once used by the Chinese - and almost certainly other cultures - to retain a connection between the living and the dead, hence the principle of ancestor-worship.

We will return to this later but for now it is enough to say that a lot more care and attention was put into grave-siting than in this case, where the ch'i was following a line going up the street and consequently richoteting backwards and forwards, restlessly. This would create a disruptive force in all the houses, not just where my clients lived.

At the time of the appointment, they confirmed what I had already discovered. They heard people walking around upstairs when there was no-one there, their neighbours had witnessed the adjoining wall 'spitting plaster out' and blamed them for it, they both often woke from hideous nightmares. It wasn't just them, they said. They knew others in the street were having problems but wouldn't discuss them.

"Are we haunted?" they asked me.

I informed them that I didn't believe in ghosts in the traditional way but that they did have a problem. I explained about the ch'i rocketing up and down the street.

"What can we do?" they asked.

"Move," I said.

I'm simplifying things considerably for there were other factors involved, but I need to make a point - namely, that you can move your furniture about as much as you like, you can activate your Wealth Corner, you can change the colour of your walls, but if the earth energies are not supportive of your endeavours then you don't stand a chance.

The Cowley Line

It may seem I have chosen mostly negative examples of lines or - to be more precise - the ways in which we tend to be living disharmoniously with them. This is true and there are two main reasons for this: one is that there are a lot of examples of disharmony with the Earth. You just have to look out your front door or at any newspaper for evidence of that. Secondly, it is in the nature of this work to be consulted when there is a 'problem' of some sort though this is not always the case - sometimes people have no trouble with where they live but wish to enhance and refine their surroundings, to take them 'to a higher level'. This last type of work is very joyful and rewarding but the rougher side of the tracks has its

Cowley Road, Oxford.

A clearly straight alignment with Cowley Road and St. Mary's in the distance.

own rewards. A case in point is a line that is probably as close to being what I call a 'black stream' as anything I've ever worked with.

Look at the map of Oxford in the previous chapter. The Cowley Line moves in a South-East/North-West orientation. For some of its path, it follows the Cowley Road - in the photograph here you can see the road pointing straight at the steeple of St Mary's Church in the distance.

Cowley Road is notorious in Oxford for many things. Whenever I gave a talk in that city, if I felt the audience were getting sleepy I would just mention 'Cowley Road' and interest was piqued to the extent of everybody vociferously disagreeing or agreeing with everybody else. This area is as far removed from the 'dreaming spires' of tourist-friendly Oxford as you can get, yet for those who live there and have formed a bond with this so-called poor area of the city it has a richness, excitement and depth missing elsewhere in the city. One client (and this line has given me many clients) has a poster in her house with a picture of Oxford and a Wordsworth quotation: 'Nature never did betray the heart that loved her'. This sentiment is key not just for the Cowley Line but for others too.

Let's just take a look at some of the places in the line's vicinity. The flow seems to be from South-East to North-West, so the first point on the line here is a car factory, followed by:

Temple Cowley - named after an old stomping ground of
   the Knights Templar
(St Bartholomews Chapel + Well - an old healing place
   used for lepers)
St John's Church
Cowley Road
St Clements - once an old church and a gateway to Oxford
St Mary's Church
St Barnabas Church in Magdalen Street
(Blackfriars Monastery)
Jericho
St Barnabas church
Binsey Well - a famous old healing well
Wytham Abbey and Wytham Wood

Those in (brackets) are points which are up to half a kilometre from the straight course of the line.

There is nothing at first sight here to warn one of anything being amiss, though the gigantean bulk of a car factory being dumped right on top of the line might sound a few alarms. Most of the clues come from talking to people who live in the vicinity about past occurrences and from actually touching the line, as described earlier. One clue emerged quite quickly when I was told that two of the streets - one by Cowley Road, the other in Jericho and known popularly as the 'bunny-run' - were once notorious for their prostitutes.

But the main indication came from actually getting to know the line's ch'i. What I picked up almost immediately was the colour 'green' and a sense of matriarchy, of it being a very powerful 'female' line.

So returning to the key question - to what extent is the situation above the line expressing that nature? - I looked at the car factory (and we all know which gender it is that tends to be obsessed with cars), at the university (which only recently even allowed women to join) and at the churches (phallic symbols of what is indisputably a patriarchal religion - or if you want to be politely Feng Shui about it, the pointing spires are of the most yang element, Fire, and placed on a yin line).

The research didn't stop there, but it all kept coming back to the same theme: the male suppressing the female. No wonder 'she' was unhappy.

The pressures resulting from this imbalance would be mitigated somewhat by the presence of other lines. For example, the two lines shown on an approximate North-South orientation and crossing the Cowley Road originate from very watery areas to the North and their presence seem to have a 'soothing' effect on the Cowley Line as they themselves are in good health. This is only true for a limited area though and to a limited extent.

Since discovering and working with the Cowley Line I have found it representative of Oxford on a larger scale, that of a matriarchal energy forced to be something else. Even the name given to a stretch of the Thames within the city is 'Isis' - the fact that it is supposed to be a derivative of the old name 'Thamesis' and not the Egyptian goddess doesn't matter when we are working on a symbolic level of 'clues'.

So how to proceed once we have found the source of such malaise? The answer is surprisingly simple and takes us quite neatly to the next chapter:

Once we have discovered the nature of such a line we check to see if that nature is being expressed - or repressed.

In the case of the Cowley Line it is a question of to what extent its feminine principle is being allowed to flourish. Put simply, whether a woman living on the line is compromising in any way whatsoever in order to fit into male ideas. If she doesn't compromise then the line responds and she is 'blessed'. For a man the issue is also around feminine issues - Is he in touch with his feminine side? Does he feel scared around women? Does he attempt to control them in any way?

The joy of living in harmony with a line is tremendous, which I why I often encourage clients to get to know the lines in their vicinity deeply. Sometimes this is happening already, instinctively. Irmela, whom we met before in Chapter Three, was flourishing in resonance with the Cowley Line, which passed right through her garden. (She was the one who had the Wordsworth quotation displayed proudly in her house.) All my research could contribute was a more conscious awareness on her part, for she had already fallen 'in tune' with the line.

Sampford Courtney, Devon

In most cases a road will be healthier and more life-enhancing if meandering whilst following a line, such as in this village on the edge of Dartmoor.

Somebody else on the line - in Jericho - suddenly discovered that she had green fingers. "It's incredible," she told me. "I've never been able to grow anything in my life but suddenly every plant I touch flourishes." She then went on to paint ivy and other climbers on the walls of her basement kitchen, creating a beautiful, soft, tranquil oasis in the core of the city. Irmela, in her own way, had experienced something similar. She returned from the supermarket on Cowley Road one day with a bag of cherries. She spat one of the stones out into the back garden. That stone is now a magnificent cherry tree that she never had to tend and it also completes the 'missing corner' of the house.

Both of these people had - on some level - said to the line 'I want to work with you' and the Earth had responded with its own individual song for that place.

Related Reading

The Songlines	Bruce Chatwin	(Jonathan Cape)
Spiritual Dowsing	Sig Lonegren	(Gothic)
Strange Oxford	Chris Morgan	(Golden Dawn)

Chapter 6

Healing the Dragon

Tao abides in non-action.
Yet nothing is left undone.
If kings and lords observed this,
The ten thousand things would develop naturally.

Lao Tzu

Wu Wei

People often inquire 'What can you do?' about an imbalance in earth energies. My usual reply is something like 'As little as possible' which causes a fair bit of consternation.

There is a fondness amongst Feng Shui practitioners to broadcast their success stories. This is not surprising, because there are a lot of success stories in Feng Shui regardless of what school you adhere to and also because it's a great ego-massage to tell everyone about them. I'm not immune to this for I personally love a good ego-massage; but I often prefer disaster stories because they can be even more interesting and a lot can be learned from them. Experienced dowsers are likely to read the following 'Sorcerer's Apprentice' account with horror.

In the beginning of my taking note of earth energies and their sometimes adverse effects on people I was at a loss as to what action to take. I knew what was happening but not what to do about it.

The diagram overleaf shows a school I worked at in England. The West-East line I had explored thoroughly. There were a lot of interesting points to this one, not least of which was its tendency to only be active during the hunting season and switched 'off' in the summer. It also passed through a popular hunting meet and a pub named after a well-known hunter. A builder who worked in the area was also a dowser and had the less esoteric explanation that the line switched 'on' when the water table was high.

But it is the line moving from North to South that was causing problems because it ran through the new extension on the North side of the building. This wasn't the only problem - you may notice just how strong the White Tiger side of the school is with the extension, for example - but it was the one I felt I might be able to work with.

I got hold of a few books on dowsing. After some reading I came across the 'stake in the line' approach for moving a line. With great enthusiasm I dowsed for the exact position of the line on both sides of the building. Aiming for the 'heart'

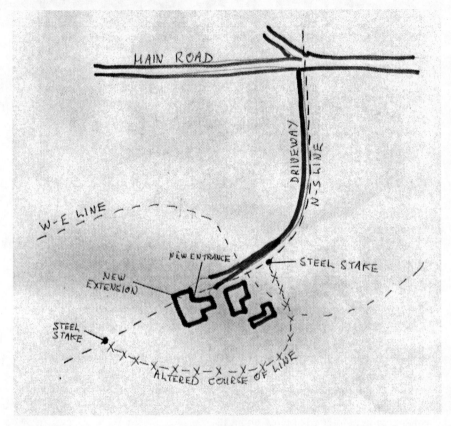

Note the curving nature of the lines, which is more evident at this scale.
Sketch reproduced from the author's field notes.

of the line at the points marked on the map, I drove steel stakes deep into the earth. The advice I read said I had to 'ask permission' of the line to do so. Well, I asked and in the absence of any obvious answer I took it as a 'yes'.

The next day I dowsed and found that the line had moved, in a new, meandering direction around the building. It was a success! Or not.

I didn't tell anyone what I'd done but within the next weeks reports were pouring in from various people of strange goings on along the adjacent driveway. Figures were seen in the evening, only to vanish when approached. Sometimes it was just 'feelings' of paranoia or glimpses of shadows moving in the trees. At other times it was just hilarious - two boys had been terrified by meeting a hooded figure looming out of the mist on the driveway and walking straight past them without saying a word. This later turned out to be one of the girls who was in a particularly foul mood that night.

But it was the overall atmosphere that had changed. Before, that area of the school had been neutral, not one thing or another and certainly not rife with paranoia. Feeling somewhat guilty and not knowing what to do, I kept as quiet as I could about my mistake. The effects seemed to dissipate after some months, by which time I had left the school anyway.

Later I happened to meet up with the builder who had some more work at the school. He knew what I had done and informed me that the line had eventually just 'snapped' back to its previous course. I had a chance to check this later and he was perfectly correct.

This was one of the biggest lessons I ever learnt and through it I came to develop an appreciation of non-action, a principle referred to in Chinese as wu wei.

Forde Abbey, Somerset

Builders of the past instinctively took care of the lung mei by either avoiding them or creating space for them to breathe, such as with this archway which has a line passing underneath. Irish builders used to place sticks upright at the corners of proposed foundations: if any stick were knocked down overnight the assumption was that it was on a Fairy Path and a different location woulkd then be tried.

In the modern world, and in the West particularly, there is a stigma about doing nothing. 'Idle hands are the devil's workshop' etc. In the East though, the ability to sit still and do nothing can indicate depth of meditation. Zazen in Japan involves sitting and staring at a blank wall. In comparison, even Vipassana - sitting still and watching one's breath - is a highly active form of meditation.

In summary, it is my experience that the actual need to 'do something' often comes from neurosis, a desperation. If your trust in the universe is big enough you can allow it to follow its own course so that when you do actually act it is in harmony with your surroundings. Anything more than that is an imposition of your will. In retrospect, I see my driving stakes into the earth as horrendously violent. A much better way would have been to build archways or glass doors where the line meets and exits the building, as some builders knew instinctively in the past.

This is why I normally insist on just one thing when working with the lung mei: understanding. I have given some examples of how this can be achieved in the previous chapter. When this understanding is present, the Earth responds.

There is a direct analogy with people. When you have a problem that you need to talk about with someone, you will either find yourself confronted with a companion who has their own agenda and pre-determined set of rules or a companion who simply listens, without judgement. Who would you rather talk to? And who do you think the Earth would rather talk to?

A natural development with the 'hands on earth' approach with a line is - once you have surmised to the best of your abilities the qualities of the line - to ask it what it wants, how it would like to be 'represented'.

A word of warning here though: some lines are in such a state that you can't get past the sheer amount of 'noise' they're generating. When this is the case, it is absolutely essential that you pull back and don't do anything - for more research and understanding are required before you - and the line - are anywhere near ready to go further.

In the following pages we are going to look at aspects of healing the Earth and ourselves, but I cannot emphasise enough the importance of non-action. The first and foremost principle is understanding. So that when you do act it is with totality and whole-heartedness, not just because you 'think it is a good idea'.

If in doubt, do nothing.

Guided Meditation

Many people who become interested in healing the energies of their environment also become interested in using various forms of guided meditation in order to do so. This almost certainly cannot do any harm and is as close to the principle of wu wei as possible yet still showing an intent of goodwill.

I myself use something similar, as described at the end of the chapter, but I see it more as a guided fantasy, a technique by which you can establish an imaginative connection with a place, hopefully sowing the seeds for a more grounded connection.

Some people work very efficiently with these methods and but there are also places I know that have supposedly been 'cured' by people using guided meditation yet in actuality very little, if anything, changed. Sometimes good intent is not enough, which is where the pragmatism of Feng Shui can be an advantage.

Yin and Yang Balance

Understanding the nature of a line will give you plenty of insight as to what is happening on its course. The examples in the previous chapter should already have made that clear. Intrinsic to this understanding is the concept of yin and yang. Much has been written about this elsewhere so I am not going to reiterate statements about something that is both so simple and so profound.

With the lung mei it is not a question of establishing a universal balance in the yin/yang; rather, it is finding the balance that is natural for each line. The Death Line was yin and perfectly happy; the Active Line was yang and unhappy, having to deal with energies that were totally inappropriate for it; the Cowley Line was yin but expressing a disharmony that was reflected elsewhere in the city.

Sometimes there is harmony present but hidden within apparent disharmony.

A student of mine was following a line with me once in the countryside near Oxford. I was showing her the 'stalking' and 'hands on earth' techniques. The photograph overleaf shows part of the line where it manifests as a straight path by a church.

I knew this line was extremely yang and not in a healthy state. I had got an impression of male violence when I'd studied it before but I hadn't told my student this. When she dowsed for the centre of the line and put her hands on the earth there, she felt immediately terrified.

"Male hands pushing my face into the dirt," she said, hurriedly walking away from the spot.

We were both feeling very uptight and serious but what was particularly interesting was that what I was experiencing as simply uncomfortable she, as a woman, found immensely distressing. This showed the value of working with more than just oneself - and particularly with both sexes.

The next interesting point was half-a-mile along the line when I spotted a group of oak trees near the path. Having read that oaks often grow above underground streams I went to have a look for signs of geopathic stress (which we will be looking at in the next section). To my amusement I found the area inundated with mole hills - not just a few, but hundreds. Somehow this was very funny.

My companion came over to join me and burst out laughing. We were both under the impression that the moles were having a party.

There were no lines that we found in this area but the yin qualities of the

The path and alignment with gates in the distance shows the 'uptight' area of the line, the geopathic stress area with the moles and oak trees being over the horizon in the dustance.

geopathic stress were balancing the yang of the line. We could summarise it like this:

The Line: Yang, serious, uptight, 'keeping it together', 'got a job to do'.
The Geopathic Stress: Yin, funny, 'lighten up', 'let's have a party'.

Sound familiar? I think we all know quite a few relationships like this and we can often spot this same dichotomy in ourselves.

It was clear that the solution to the imbalance would be to get the two to 'talk to each other'.

The implication of the 'node' points at the Caduceus, where the two serpents coincide, is obvious but what that means in practical terms is not. I feel we are more at the point now of rediscovering ways of healing and until our knowledge and experience is sufficient it is by far better to be patient and to learn. In the meantime much of the yin/yang balance can be regained through direct and simple means ie by respecting the individuality of each line.

Geopathic Stress

Geopathic Stress, or GS as it is sometimes affectionately referred to by practitioners, is often seen as the bête noire of Feng Shui. Again, as is the wont in modern man, things are often made out to be much more complicated than necessary.

Geopathic Stress occurs when there is an instability in the earth itself underneath a building. This can be caused by underground water, caverns or even crystals. This usually leads to a very yin site, too yin for living quarters.

There are psychological clues for GS: occupants in an effected building can become morose, depressive, their immune systems may suffer with them becoming prone to virtually any passing bug.

Spirit of the Dance

The behaviour of trees can often indicate what is happening underground, twisting branches responding to the raw ch'i of geopathic stress. Whether this is grotesque or beautiful depends largely on point of view. Similarly, with humans involved, the stress can lead to weakened immune systems; or, as in the case with Delphi in Greece, to enhanced meditation.

Photograph: Premgit

Some animals and plants thrive with GS and can serve as outer indications of this problem. Here are some of them:

Fauna	Flora
cats	oaks
moles	herbs
wasps	mushrooms
ants	willow
beetles	ivy
bacteria	ash
	mistletoe
	elder

This doesn't mean that if you have a happy cat you also have GS! But if you and your house have been 'adopted' by a stray cat then you may want to look into this possibility. It is also possible that your cat prefers to sleep in particular places of your house where GS is present. Other animals will tend to avoid such areas.

There is an old Russian technique for checking a proposed site to see if it has GS. This involves laying pieces of meat in a grid formation across the land. If any pieces decay with particular rapidity then those are where the GS is.

A German technique is to place an ants nest on the land. If the ants stay, then you have GS; if not, then all is clear.

But what do you do if the house is already built and you have got GS?

Well, often you have to move.

A slightly less drastic and slightly less expensive way is to employ the services of somebody who has some expertise in this area. GS practitioners are becoming quite commonplace. "Feng Shui is so five minutes ago," as one newspaper said. There are definitely well-experienced individuals in this field but I am sometimes troubled by the tendency of some to find GS in every innocent corner of every building and then to sell strange otherworldly devices to 'correct' the GS.

If the GS is not too drastic then there are two basic directions you can go in in order to work with it.

The key is actually totally in spirit with Feng Shui, in that the object is not to fight and control nature but to be in harmony with it. Part of the Chinese word for sha is Hou - depicted by four vertical lines under one horizontal. This means 'fire' and represents a destructive force rising from underneath.

Actions

Action 1: The first possibility is that as you have this energy affecting what is above the ground, the task is to transform it so that it is more acceptable to human life. This is very possibly what those expensive devices do but I've also enjoyed success using quartz crystals. Amethyst seems to be the best for this, though why, I don't know. Basically, anything that refines the energies will do the job. Dowsing or intuition will tell you where to place the crystals or devices. Another form of refinement is guided meditation, but for that to be successful you will probably need a practitioner experienced in this.

Action 2: The second option is to allow the Earth to express itself, in fact to encourage it. A few pubs in Devon were built on top of old wells. If the landlords had simply decided to hide them, they would have had GS. Instead, they made them a feature in the pub, having them well-lit and covered with glass instead of floorboards so that you can peer down into them.

If the actual physical source of the stress cannot be featured, you can consider doing so symbolically. A house on a hill that is inundated with underground streams may have difficulty actually accessing that water, in which case a fountain can be built in the front garden. (Water at the back is, generally, not a good idea as it brings instability to a place from which you need support.)

I have often worked and stayed on houseboats on the English canals. The movement of ch'i from the Water element to the Wood of the boat is very harmonious; with metal boats the movement is in the other direction - from Metal to Water - and this often suits healers or other people, such as teachers, who are more intent on giving something to the environment rather than making a fast buck. I have never stayed in any of those wooden houses you see raised on stilts above stretches of water in the Far East, but they also strike me as being harmonious, turning what could be a source of stress into something of beauty.

Mallorca I also find interesting in that the entire island could be considered to be suffering from geopathic stress, though I would say 'enjoying' rather than 'suffering'. There are numerous caverns throughout the island, many with crystal deposits and many with pockets of water - known locally as 'fonts ufanes' - trapped until shifts in pressure cause the water to push through tunnels and burst out at the surface. A building company I worked for there told me they often had problems where a site was considered stable yet later water would come shooting out of the ground in an unprecedented manner. Yet Mallorca is a beautiful place to live or visit, its main problem not being GS but the greed and insensitivity of wealthy investment in tourism and real estate, by enterprising locals and northern Europeans. Somehow the potential 'stress' has become something totally different, perhaps because the subterranean energies are allowed to express themselves, whether through the popular crystal caves or the water springs coming out of the earth.

We have dealt here with areas of general stress. I have done this mainly to look at GS from a slightly different perspective, but obviously there are other considerations, such as localised pockets of GS in a house or small, disturbing lines of GS. This is why there are people who specialise in such things and why dowsing becomes a necessary tool in order to understand more what we are dealing with.

In the meantime, we can summarise the three main ways of dealing with GS covered in this section:

1. Move.
2. Refine the disturbing energies.
3. Find a way to allow the Earth to express itself.

Seiki Lines

One of the most astonishing and influential books that have come my way in recent years is 'The Shamanic Healer' by Ikuko Osumi and Malcolm Ritchie, about the former's use of the almost-forgotten Japanese healing art of Seiki-Jutsu. There were many things about this book that impressed me, not least of which was Ikuko Osumi's keen intuitive sense of when an object in a house was in an incorrect position, but I found it particularly interesting that she would look for what she called a 'Seiki Line' in a house, which is where she would choose to do the healing.

It seemed clear to me that she was actually utilising the natural healing energies of the Earth via the smaller lines of ch'i. I realised from this that while I had been happily stomping around, dramatically following the larger dragon and tiger lines, I'd neglected to pay attention to the quieter, more humble energies that are around.

Having read the book, I was encouraged to start seeking what I shall here refer to as 'Seiki Lines', though elsewhere I have referred to them as 'capillaries'. Using dowsing and similar techniques as before - seeking patterns is difficult at such a scale but the concentration of ch'i is still apparent - I discovered that these lines were pretty much ubiquitous. Every house is likely to have at least one passing through.

One house I visited had had a survey done by a Geopathic Stress consultant and the occupant was told that she had a GS line passing through her bed, which was why she had trouble sleeping. I found the same line but it was a perfectly healthy Seiki line - it was just the high levels of ch'i that were disturbing my client. My advice remained the same though, which was simply to move the bed half-a-metre away.

Awareness of Seiki lines has influenced me in two main ways:

First, to become more sensitive to the subtler ch'i affecting a site - and to ensure that a line is not excessively blocked eg through very heavy furniture or clutter.

Secondly, working on the principle of encouraging the Earth to express itself, sensitivity to a line can influence what it is that you choose to decorate the house with in those areas crossed by the line. For example, if you use the 'hands on earth' technique with the line and get the impression of particular colours, then find a way to incorporate those colours into your interior design.

Seiki healing itself I have not experienced, although where I'm staying now everyone prefers to have the dining table placed over a line - and I'm sure we"re all eating very healthily on every level! - and I possibly did experience a similar type of healing not long ago, courtesy of a very powerful line - and a seal.

Seal Line

One day I woke up and I could hardly walk. My lower back had gone out of alignment. I was in excruciating pain and getting even to the next room was difficult. To compound the difficulties I had to drive several hundred miles to Cornwall, where I was leading a workshop in a few days' time.

On the drive down I stopped with some friends in Devon, one of whom was trained in the Alexander Technique. He managed to get me walking a bit better but only a bit. About a hundred metres was my limit.

Soon after arriving in Cornwall, the friend who had organised the workshop took me to a beach which involved a short walk down a steep incline.

I was relaxing against the cliff-edge by the water, wondering how I was going to get back up the hill (as I'd failed miserably with such a slope the day before), when I noticed something peculiar: just in front of me where the waves were lapping the beach, the seaweed had formed a distinct box-like pattern. Nowhere else along the beach was it like this. Having had my attention, caught this way, I looked closer and saw a subtle shifting of the light. It was as if there were a density of bright colours in that place, mostly of a golden yellow hue.

I hobbled away to get a distant perspective. I realised there was a band of light emanating from the cliff where I'd been standing - I was actually seeing a line moving straight out to sea, exactly where the seaweed-pattern had formed. I had caught glimpses of this effect before but never so blatantly.

"There's a line there, isn't there?!" called out my friend from further along the beach. "I didn't want to say anything to prejudice you - but I can actually see it!"

I lay down for a while on the sand where the line crossed. A bit later I looked up to see a shape bobbing along in the waves exactly where the line went. It was a seal, just floating, looking half-asleep.

Nothing else happened, as the seal hardly moved, but the surprising result of all this was that twenty minutes later I could almost run up the hill.

My rejuvenation lasted for the next few days, enabling me to lead the workshop comfortably. Afterwards though, the pain returned and I found myself going back to the beach, which was empty - except for the seal which was in the same place.

I lay alternately on the beach and against the rock once more. And once again I made it back up the hill easily.

This became a daily routine. The seal started to take notice of me fairly early on, because we were usually the only two there. Once he (I always felt it was a 'he' though I don't know why) swam closer to get a good look at me. Another time a second seal - whom I instinctively labelled a 'she' - approached and tried to get his attention, but he just wasn't interested and clearly preferred to just float. As if bored after five minutes, she swam away. At this stage I began to get the distinct impression he was there for the same reason as me - healing.

After a week or two of this it became time for me to leave Cornwall. My back was now nearly back to normal and I knew the process was complete. I went back to the beach for a farewell, but I wasn't surprised to find it empty for the first time. The process was over for both of us.

My back did need chiropractor treatment in the long run, but the time with the seal gave me enough ' healing ch'i' to get on with for quite a while afterwards.

The line itself was observable on maps stretching for several miles and, because of this largely-undeveloped area of England, is in perfectly good health.

A connection between the lung mei and wildlife is often remarked upon and I have alluded to it a few times in this book. Cloven-hoofed animals are particularly known to follow lines and male deer are thought to battle over power-points (ie where several lines converge) in order to decide on the right of sovereignty over those areas.

Those familiar even slightly with Native American culture are probably aware of the direct connection with animals and the particular 'Medicine' they each represent.

Crop Circles

These spectacular formations in crop fields have mostly been recorded in England since the late 1980's. There are numerous books on them, all - with some notable exceptions - keen to hammer home their authors' own particular theories, ranging from aliens to drunks. Personally, I don't care who or what is doing them - even if it's drunk aliens - but I am very much interested in the effect they have on the Earth and what is written in these pages is not meant to trumpet yet another theory, but to encourage you to find out more for yourself.

It is clear though that, whoever is responsible for these formations, they get around. Not only are formations frequently recorded in Holland, Germany, America and other places, but I was also in Switzerland when I received a phonecall from some people living by the Alps: they had woken up to find two mysterious circles in the field outside their house.

There are theories that it is the Earth itself doing the formations. Again, this doesn't interest me unduly as there is plenty of contradictory evidence to that as well, but the effect is quite tangible - even casual visitors to the formations tend to be affected, sometimes through nausea (migraines, dizziness etc.), sometimes with what is referred to in New Age circles as 'bliss attacks'. Other people, of course, are overwhelmed with strong uncontrollable feelings of cynicism.

My interest initially was very much as a tourist. I enjoyed the formations in Wiltshire over the years but wasn't so much investigating as simply visiting them as one would an art gallery. It was when I was walking along the hill opposite the 1995 formation known as the 'DNA formation' that I noticed something under my feet, directly in line with the centre of the 'helix'.

It was an extremely intense concentration of ch'i, a dragon line. Putting my hands on the ground, I sensed it as a straight golden line coming from the heart of the formation and extending far beyond. It felt vibrant, active to a degree I'd never met before. My impression was that it was healing the earth. To this day I don't know why it was straight as outside the crop circle phenomenon I hadn't known this before, despite reading accounts of straight, yang 'energy leys' as in Sig Lonegren's work.

I had a second chance to test this effect a year later.

I knew from the Internet that two new formations had appeared near Swindon, the first of the season and in rape crop. The first was a cog-like shape and the second seemed clearly to be one that had been copied by somebody out of a textbook as it was a fairly accurate rendition of the Kabbalistic Tree of Life. Nevertheless, I wanted to vist both of them as they were in close proximity to each other.

The 'cog' I could see immediately as I drove up the hill adjacent to it, but the Tree of Life was nowhere to be found. I parked at the top where there were foundations of an ancient hillfort. The weather was extremely foul. Nobody else was walking in the howling wind and rain, but I'd come enough of a distance not to want to give up; so I walked around as much of the hill as possible, attempting to see the missing formation - but to no avail.

Before giving up entirely, I went to the centre of the castle and dowsed for any lines that might be converging there. Astonishingly, apart from the usual convergence at such points of lines of various types and hue, there were two golden lines, bright and effervescent with energy. One was coming straight from the 'cog' formation, I knew, so the second had to be from the Tree of Life.

I followed this second line for a kilometre or two before finding the formation nestled in a field at the base of the hill.

From that point on I started to care less about who or what was responsible for these formations. Whoever they are they are participating in a healing process that is commendable and have made many peoples' lives a lot richer in quality in that process.

This is not always the case. It is well-known that at least some of th formations are done by 'artists', if not all. These people are also known to dowse for the best sites so that dowsers can be fooled effectively, which I find pretty mysterious in itself! But one formation in 1998 seemed in direct opposition to the benificent effects experienced with others.

It was done in the shape of a pentagram. The first thing I found unusual was that I couldn't find it. I knew the area it was in but there were no outer indications and dowsing simply revealed a blank. I only found it hours later after being told where it was. On arriving, I met the farmer whose field it was in. He told me how he had been woken up in the night by a car driving away from the field, too fast for him to get its number plate. In the formation itself, the atmosphere was markedly different from how I had experienced it in others - the visitors seemed unhappy, serious, and I was more aware of the pesticide on the crop brushing against my skin than anything.

Even though the formation was much publicised for its excellence, I always found that a shallow assessment afterwards. Whoever was responsible hadn't done a good job in my opinion.

A difference between a 'good' and a 'bad' formation can be experienced by almost anyone directly by walking around inside one, for in many ways crop circles are modern day equivalents of sacred labyrinths. It's more important to experience them directly rather than theorise about them: to walk the talk, not talk the walk. In this manner you are not pursuing an abstract idea of a key but actually entering and becoming the key itself. This can be done to some extent through meditation rather than having to physically visit each site. As with drawings of sacred labyrinths, you can experience something of the specialness of a crop circle by tracing its course with your finger on a picture of it.

The comparison with sacred geometry is obvious and has been noted by many researchers. This could well be the way forward in the future as regards healing the Earth but I would be very cautious at utilising geometry until we really know what we are doing - examples of our propensity to meddle and end up doing more harm than good are legion. Somehow the circle makers have usually gotten away with it, perhaps through superior knowledge, perhaps through instinct, intuition, luck or guidance.

In the meantime I would like to finish this section with a comment from a different perspective.

It was the end of the summer near Avebury one year when I stood in a vast formation, a beautiful fractal of circles, dancing and spiralling in an overall pattern that couldn't be comprehended fully at ground level. Even so, it was an impressive sight.

I was alone but for an English man and his Greek girlfriend, who had travelled from London just to see this. We all three were in awe, standing in silence under the gradually darkening sky, when the farmer approached.

We went to talk with him.

"What do you think about having this geometry in your field?!" the girl asked him enthusiastically.

"I don't care if it's humans or aliens. They're buggers whoever they are," was the answer.

Dragon Heart

Near where you are now there will be a place that is particularly strong with earth energies. Usually this will be within about ten kilometres - if it is further than that then it is likely that the area you are in is rather depleted with ch'i - 'lacking in energy'.

This special place is known as a Dragon Heart, in Western Geomancy sometimes referred to as a Power Point. It can be synonymous with a Dragon Pulse (converging ridge-lines) but not necessarily. Often Dragon Hearts are indicated in other ways, such as by a sacred site, a standing stone, a hill in a flat

Dragon Heart

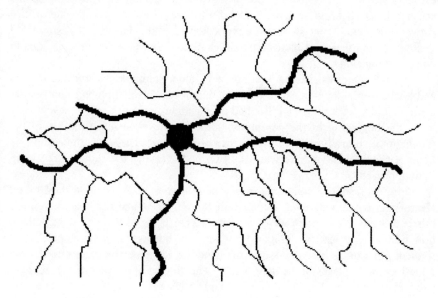

How a Dragon Heart nourishes an area via the lung mei.

landscape or a folkloric memory of it being a magical place - but the underlying factor will be that many lines will meet there. In India this is where you may find a teerth: a garden where Earth and Heaven meet, a place where humanity can walk with the Divine. (Teerths, however beautifully designed, if they are not placed on a powerful ch'i spot will lack that special, elusive 'magical' feeling.)

People who have lived somewhere for a long time often know immediately where their Dragon Heart is. Newcomers have to search for it - or perhaps be guided to it.

The Dragon Heart is the major source of ch'i for the area. If the connections - via the lung mei - to it are weak or have to 'pump' the ch'i too far then there is a problem. The Feng Shui practitioners of old, the Dragon Men, would sometimes reactivate the ch'i by running from a Dragon Pulse to the place on which they were working.

Ancient ceremonies often act out something similar, on a yearly basis. In Burghead, North Scotland, the Celtic New Year is still celebrated by a midnight ceremony of a man running through the streets, carrying burning coals in a brazier, and followed by the entire town's populace to the peak of a hill overlooking the sea. It is an unforgettable experience for anyone who has attended it. There are similar ceremonies throughout the world, not all at night though, nor all necessarily so dramatic.

Anna Halprin in 'The Power of Place' tells the amazing story of how she and her group of dancers, with the compliance of the town, effectively reclaimed a mountain from the pervasive influence of a killer. The mountain had, as she explains, become their 'shadow' after a series of murders in 1979, creating such a sense of terror that no-one dared walk on it for two years. In fact, the authorities actively discouraged it. It was in a workshop of Anna Halprin's that supressed feelings about the loss of their mountain came to the surface and they decided to do something about it.

By leading a procession up the mountain, along with various spiritual leaders and townspeople, they managed to break the taboo the situation had imposed on them. Within two weeks the killer had been caught.

At the beginning of the ceremony, some people were led, running up the mountain in four directions. It is interesting that what they understood as being a coastal Native American tradition is essentially the same as the Feng Shui approach.

During workshops I sometimes use visualisation to take people to the Dragon Hearts near where they live. I encourage them to relax and just see where their mind takes them, with often surprising results. On 'bringing them back' I ask them how best to represent the Dragon Heart in their homes - sometimes nothing is needed, other times an alteration in the decor or, if the person is an artist, some quite incredible pieces of art may result. The similarity between this technique and that of stalking a line is clear - often you will be following the lung mei to and from the Heart, either physically or mentally.

In summary:

Find the Dragon Heart of your area - there may even be more than one.
Establish a connection with it by walking a line to and from it, or by using guided fantasy.
If necessary, reactivate it through running or by way of a ceremony.

The main thing, though, is to know your Heart.

Related Reading

It's Not Too Late	Hamish Miller	(Penwith)
Labyrinths	Sig Lonegren	(Gothic)
Medicine Cards	Jamie Sams/David Carson	(Bear & Co.)
The Power of Place	James A. Swan	(Gateway)
Safe As Houses?	David Cowan & Rodney Girdlestone	(Gateway)
The Shamanic Healer	Ikuko Osumi/Malcolm Ritchie	(Century)

Chapter 7

Spirits of the Land

*Meanwhile, the river of wild jaguars flowed
below the surface of our hungry roads.*

Ben Okri, 'The Famished Road'

Symbols and Weather Ch'i

Having read this far - or simply by having some interest in Feng Shui, earth mysteries or related subjects - you are probably quite comfortable already with the concept of ch'i or prana, an 'energy' that is notoriously difficult to define yet once you know what it is you simply know. When dealing with very practical issues, such as traffic or energy efficiency in homes, it is very easy to translate ch'i into more obvious terms, a fact I have been happy to exploit when working with architects or builders. Problems arise though when moving into more paranormal areas, where there is no avoiding terms such as 'ghost' or 'entity', not only because of the threat they impose to any rationalism but also because of the vagueness of such terms, ie what do they actually mean?

It is not possible to give a definitive answer to this, partly because these names refer to many types of phenomena but also because it is not possible to limit them and to what they refer. In the West people are accustomed, with a fondness for dualistic thought, in thinking in terms of the 'Known' and the 'Unknown', where the latter is simply 'waiting to be known'. In India there is also a third category: the Unknowable. This shows an ease with Mystery, something the West has to rediscover. In American and European stories the scientist or the detective nearly always solves the mystery. This attitude has also characterised research into earth mysteries, with a desperation to 'solve the riddle' at all costs so that there is no mystery. The truth is that some of it will be solved but much of it never can be. In Feng Shui terms, the Water element, like the breath of the Dragon, is manifesting as mist where shapes are indistinct and we are moving in perpetual twilight.

Another block for the modern intellectual is an inability to really understand symbols. D.H. Lawrence is one of the few white men I know of who has made an issue out of the fact that we have been guilty of reducing symbols to meanings. His strongest example was of the Egyptian ankh. If you ask anybody who knows anything about symbols what the ankh stands for they will say something like, 'eternal life'. Lawrence's point was that we have now reduced something that is vast and mysterious to a mere label, whereas if a powerful symbol is lived and understood from a total perspective, not just a mental one, it will be impossible to find words to describe it.

This is relevant to understanding the symbols nature gives us too. In Feng Shui weather ch'i is seen as being intermediary between earth and celestial ch'i: that is, representative of what is going on between earth and cosmic forces. We have already looked at various meanings for points of the compass and Native American belief can interpret wind direction accordingly. The violent thunderstorm during the climax of a ghost story is a popular form of weather symbolism; and the wild storm in Shakespeare's 'Macbeth' symbolises a dramatic and ominous shift of events in the play. In both Native American and Indian cultures there is mention sometimes of a 'dark wind' sweeping through people's souls, causing them to act with irrational destructiveness. Any boundary between inner and outer realities becomes vague at this point but a certain level of detachment is still vital - for sometimes a thunderstorm is just a thunderstorm and strong awareness is needed in order to be intelligent about symbolism and not get carried away.

This doesn't mean that we abandon the need for meaning in symbolism - on the contrary, a meaning gives us something we can use - just that we are capable of going beyond that.

By all means let us solve that which is simply Unknown, but also be insistent on recognising the Unknowable when we face it. In the following pages we are going to oscillate between the two quite frantically, so: enjoy the ride.

Cats and Dogs

In 1996 a Venezuelan friend looked puzzled after coming back from a walk in the North Devon countryside.

"You don't have panthers in this country, do you?" she asked.

"No," was the answer. "Why?"

"Because I've just seen one," she said.

She had seen similar creatures in South America but couldn't quite believe her own eyes in this case, not knowing that she was only one of many who had seen the famous Beast of Exmoor in that particular area.

At the time of writing, news reports in the West Country of England are full of reports about 'big cat' sightings: supposedly a lion, a lioness and a puma have all been sighted in recent months. This is not new and has gone on for some time, but it is only now that reports have reached such an impressive frequency. In late 1998 at 1 a.m. I myself witnessed what looked and behaved exactly like a lion cub jumping around, clearly lit by my car's headlights, only a few metres ahead of me before it dived through a hedge.

Common consent is that all these animals have been released from private zoos since the Dangerous Wild Animals Act of 1976 and have been breeding ever since.

We have looked earlier at the suggestion of understanding animal symbols but few people in England would be quite prepared to have to come to terms with lions - symbolic or otherwise - in their backyard!

That adaptability is important in this work is obvious but there are times when the animal in question seems to cross the boundary of what is considered 'real' and the researcher may experience discomfort at this point, as I did when considering the unfeasibility of lions roaming the English countryside. The wildlife expert Trevor Beer, when investigating the 'Beast of Exmoor' turned up plenty of convincing evidence as to its tangibility but was puzzled to come across testimonies of more paranormal behaviour.

Having read his book in the early 90's, I was intrigued by one story of a driver on Exmoor who had met not a big cat but a hound at some crossroads. The beast was so big it looked over the vehicle's bonnet at him before vanishing.

A suspicion dawned on me that we were dealing not necessarily with a flesh-and-blood animal but with some unknown elemental force from the earth itself. To investigate, I retraced the driver's journey until I reached the crossroads he had described in his account. I then got out of the car and searched in the fields adjacent to the road where, sure enough, I found a large Bronze Age barrow in one of them. It was only months later I came across the folkloric belief that ghostly black dogs guarded treasure in these places.

An obvious question to ask is: Are we therefore dealing with supernatural entities or not?

Well, sometimes we are, sometimes we're not. It doesn't matter. We are more concerned here with whether they have symbolic significance or not. Patrick Harpur in 'Daimonic Reality', using a similar tone to Lawrence, sees it as part of the modern malaise that we are so eager to divide things into 'fact' and 'fantasy', a distinction that did not exist once upon a time. This dichotomy is clear with farmers in Devon trying to kill the Beast with rifles while others state that it is a spirit seeking revenge on modern farming methods. A more comfortable ease with paradox is apparent if you hear Tibetans or Nepalese talking about the yeti.

OVERLEAF: Famous Beast

The Beast of Exmoor provided plenty of news copy and does to this day, along with its friends in other parts of the country. These extracts are from the North Devon Journal, with thanks.

Shotgun farmers stalk a South Molton killer

'BIG CAT' HUNTER

30 lambs die on one farm

BY TIM ABBOTT

Village alert for cat-like beast

10.4.97

SETTING OFF: Last minute advice to farmer marksmen from Mr. Eric Ley (right) as they leave Drewstone Farm to hunt the sheep killer.

Thursday, March 9, 1995

Exmoor beast's night on TV

By GRAHAM ANDREWS

Puma-like

■ Gathering of the guns: This was the scene in April 1982 at Drewstone Farm, near South Molton, had been slaughtered by a 'big, black and cattle animal." It was the first beast scare since

The vagueness and interchangeability of labels are common factors as we move into these twilight realms. A village called Black Dog and associated with such a phantom creature was once called Black Boy, which puzzled the researcher who told me this no end. Interestingly, a weather phenomenon known as the Morchard Bishop Depression passes right over the village. The depression is the cause of much fascination amongst meteorologists as it is purely local: oscillating between Morchard Bishop and nearby Witheridge. If you follow the depression's movement, allowing a large 'band width' (remember the Lizard's Back in Chapter Four) not only does it pass over Black Dog but, if it continued over Exmoor to the North in a straight line, would sweep - firstly, over the crossroads where the motorist had encountered the phantom hound and, secondly, several favourite haunts of the Exmoor Beast.

As we progress and the distinction between inner and outer becomes even more vague, be aware that when you are following a dragon line you are also going on an inner journey, not just an outer one; and it is helpful to remain calm no matter what manner of creature you come across.

Black Dog Lines

Soon after my discovery of the association of barrows with black dog legends, I became quite interested in similar legends and stories in other parts of Devon. Investigating a village called Down St Mary, where there was a black dog association, I also found nearby an old road by a place called Stopgate Cross where the phantom beast was also supposedly seen on frequent occasions. I then managed to trace such sightings in a straight line right across Devon.

Unfortunately for my ego I later discovered that I wasn't the first to work all this out. Earlier in the century a Mrs Barbara Carbonell had drawn out exactly the same line, guided by local accounts of sightings. Villagers who encountered the dog had the intelligence not to interfere with it and consequently no harm was done. One man often saw it near Stopgate late at night and became accustomed to the 'gurt hound so big as a calf' running beside him. In Down St Mary people often saw the animal with its 'shining eyes' and heard sounds of crashing masonry as it passed through the schoolhouse making 'for the lane beyond'. No damage was ever found though the sound of falling stones would be heard quite clearly.

This phenomenon, as reported by many researchers, is actually worldwide, examples coming from Pennsylvania, France, Croatia, South Africa, Germany and numerous other places. My own research revealed several of what I came to know as Black Dog Lines all over Devon. What this actually is seems to dwell on the border between the Unknown and the Unknowable, but there are some patterns that can be discerned, enabling us to understand and work with this phenomenon at least to some extent.

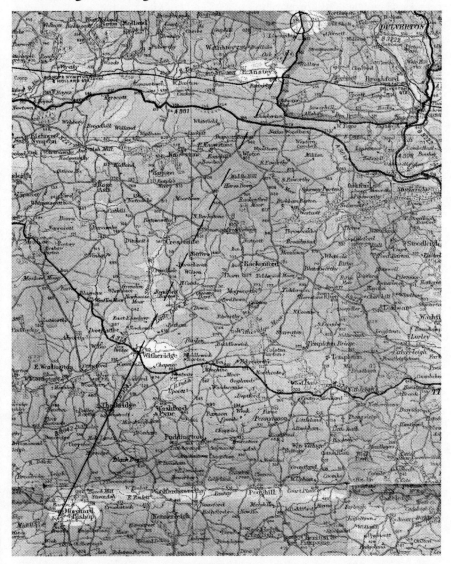

An alignment is clear between Morchard Bishop, Witheridge, East Anstey then finally the Exmoor crossroads at which the motorist encountered the phantom beast. Note the close proximity of Black Dog village to the line, where there is a parallel alignment to a castle in the South-West (not on map). Taken from the author's field notes.

In an earlier chapter I mentioned the incident in Suffolk in the sixteenth century when two dogs appeared in separate churches both killing and maiming a few people. There was initially a violent thunderstorm in Bungay, with lightning striking the parish clerk when he was cleaning the gutters of the church roof. The dog that appeared by the altar ran down the aisle and out of the church, leaving two people in close proximity dead, another shrivelled up but alive, the church clock machinery twisted and broken and claw-marks on the stones and metal of the door. The second dog, at Blythburgh seven miles away, after a similar performance left marks on the North door that are still visible today.

My way of interpreting all this is simply that these entities - whatever they are - have somewhere to get to and we sometimes get in the way, often due to badly-positioned buildings. All the accounts of these beasts verify that they do no harm unless provoked. There are numerous stories of people being badly hurt after attacking them, but otherwise the only harm seems to be when their passage is blocked such as in the case of the unfortunate worshippers in Bungay church. You can imagine, if you like, the lines the black dogs are following acting as interdimensional freeways - and nobody in their right mind parks on a freeway.

But what is the nature of a Black Dog Line and how does it affect those living in close proximity to it? Well, that varies. It is important to be clear at this point that these lines are not synonymous with black streams - they are not necessarily unhealthy nor do they need any kind of healing unless, perhaps, if they have been blocked or affected adversely somehow. A Black Dog Line can in fact do a lot to add excitement and interest to an area.

There can be problems though. The term 'black dog' in English is often used to describe unaccountable attacks of melancholy or depression and I discovered personally that there can be a connection between this condition and Black Dog Lines.

For some weeks I had been investigating one such line

Map by B. Carbonell

spanning across Devon and passing through the crossroads at Exmoor where the motorist had encountered the giant hound. A lot of interesting alignments were in evidence and I dedicated myself to the work with considerable enthusiasm.

Around this time I found myself getting extremely morose. I also started to dislike some of my friends quite intensely. I began to keep to myself more and more. Nothing seemed right. Odd things irritated me for no apparent reason.

After a month of this, meditating alone in my room, I saw in a flash what had happened: I had actually picked up something energetically from the line. It was as if something had been thrown at me and stuck, like a black cloud over my thoughts and feelings. This was a revelation. I felt immediately lighter, recognising those which were distinctly my own thoughts and those which had come from elsewhere. My relations with people improved immediately, making amends for the past month, but I was still aware of the 'cloud'.

I didn't know how to get rid of it. I contacted a well-known psychic who, after berating me for stupidly going into such areas unprotected, told me to take a valuable of some sort and to follow the line again, leaving the valuable somewhere along it.

To cut a long story short, this worked. I felt an immediate enlightening of my spirit and there was even a rainbow after I had done this! It was years later that I read of unwary travellers in Malaysia, having become sick by inadvertently following an orang bunian path, being told by witchdoctors to return and leave coins in order to appease the spirits that they had offended.

The experience of the dark cloud leaving my psyche is unforgettable. It was a very tangible phenomenon. I didn't see it as a dog but caught a glimpse of a dark shape moving away and realised I had accidentally 'caught it' through my trespass on its route.

At this point the reader may feel this phenomenon relegated comfortably to the world of spirit - or of fantasy, according to your view - but once again, paradoxes reign and I had a later experience in marked contrast to the first:

Some years after my early mapping of Black Dog Lines a friend wanted to show me an old chapel called St John's near Exeter.

"It's in ruin," he told me, "but there's also an old sacred well there. I used to have to cycle past it at night, to get home, then suddenly I didn't want to anymore. I would go an extra mile just to avoid it. I have no idea why."

It was a hot summer's afternoon when we drove to see the site. Reading the map en route, I was interested, though wary, to see that the chapel was exactly on a Black Dog Line that I'd never managed to explore fully.

The chapel ruins were on a T-junction in the middle of the countryside, next to one lonely-looking house. The main route was a straight road leading to a few houses a mile or two away to the North where there was also a high range of hills with a few isolated trees at the top of one, in direct alignment with the road. That, my friend informed me, was an old Hangman's Hill. It certainly looked the part. Locally it was also known as the Tree Graveyard because the pines planted on its crest always died.

We left the car on an adjacent track then went to view the chapel. I immediately didn't like the feel of the place. My friend agreed and we returned directly to the car.

On turning onto the long straight road, with the chapel in front and Hangman's HIll behind, my friend let out an exclamation.

He had seen something in the mirror. I turned around.

In the middle of the road, just behind us, was a large black dog just standing there. It was as if it had appeared from nowhere. It was about a metre tall. It didn't look threatening, only a bit ominous. It seemed more confused than anything.

"Let's get out of here!" yelled my friend. I had been about to get out and investigate but was suddenly aware of the foolhardiness of the idea. We didn't know what we were dealing with. We drove off rather hurriedly.

The Black Dog phenomenon contains enough material for rationalists, spiritualists and all sorts of people to chew over. Again, I wouldn't worry unduly about the various theories but instead look at what such encounters might signify. Even if the last encounter was of a flesh-and-blood beast, that doesn't alter the inherent symbolism, a clue as to the nature of the line or lines involved.

Recognising the limitations of labels, whilst still using them to the extent they are necessary, you may wish to consider the symbolism suggested: first, by wild jungle cats appearing in the middle of a country known for its pristine gardens and good manners; and, secondly, by the association of black dogs with guardianship and the fact that in the last example the animal was clearly confused and perhaps lost.

White Lady

I was on Exmoor again one day, this time to visit a site known as Five Barrows Cross. My main reason for going was to visit a standing stone nearby that was marked on the map. The location was on the crest of a hill, which would have been overlooking a large section of the moor except that there was a heavy mist that day reducing visibility to about twenty yards.

I tramped over the sodden ground, trusty compass in hand, in the direction of the barrows. From there, I counted on following bearings towards the stone that lay in an adjacent field. I wasn't far from the road when the first barrow loomed out of the mist. Walking around it, I caught glimpses of the others clustered nearby. As I was doing this, a sharp shriek caught my attention.

On a fence next to the barrow was a large white bird. The mist was too dense for me to be able to identify it. It seemed to be observing me.

Ignoring it, I took another compass bearing, consulted my map, and stomped off in the direction of the circle. Having walked a few hundred yards and traversed two fences, I found myself in an empty field with no sign of the alleged standing stone no matter how much I walked around.

Feeling at a loss of what to do, I heard that same shriek again and there was the bird, on the ground nearby, flapping its wings. I tried to approach but it flew off into the mist. Feeling somewhat defeated by the missing stone anyway, I returned to the barrows.

This time I was prepared for the sight of the white bird alighting on the fence. I looked at it and it flew off once more.

I had the distinct impression there was a significance about the encounter and about the direction the bird had flown in.

I took a compass reading of that direction, put the map down on the ground and worked out where the bird could be heading.

A few miles to the South-East, I noted, was a holy well. An alignment was apparent between the barrows and the well, so I decided to go to the latter.

I returned to my car and drove to where the well was marked on the map. Where I parked on a bridge over the little road, water was gushing down from the hills to the North. But there was more. The stream wasn't that large but around it I could sense an immense power, an energy that was pouring down from the hills and the sea in the North; the stream was just a stream, but the invisible water was a torrent. It was one of those rare occasions that ch'i was almost visible for me, not dissimilar from Australian Aboriginal paintings of the Rainbow Serpent coiled around a well or other sacred place.

The sense of power immediately began to diminish though as I followed the stream down the valley. By the time I got to where the well was supposed to be I felt no invigorating rush of energy, only a sense of despondency, of gloom.

There was no well. Only the corpses of two rotting sheep. One of the heads was moving in a grim parody of life with the activity of thousands of flies and maggots.

Feeling sick, I hurriedly left the area.

Later that year I came across what seemed to be the missing piece of the puzzle. I discovered a story about a holy well on Exmoor, above which a white lady was seen to appear on frequent occasions. The farmers who owned the land had felt so disturbed by this apparition that they'd filled in the well. The white lady was never seen again. I felt no doubt this story referred to the same well, though it is likely this story can be repeated elsewhere as well.

It is obvious that to label this apparition a 'ghost' would be to do it injustice. There is much more going on here, with the white lady possibly a representation of the once-abundant earth ch'i in that spot. There is a beauty inherent in these symbols, whether of panthers stalking the English countryside, mysterious black dogs appearing amidst thunderstorms or elegant figures appearing by wells. And how do we respond to them? We block the wells, we pour concrete over our sacred paths, chemicals into the soil - and we denounce the hidden ways of our world as 'rubbish' and then we make them so.

It is worth considering the general pattern being revealed on a world-wide scale when we group strange ecological and otherworldly occurrences together: the disturbing chupacabra 'goat-sucker' in Brazil and Mexico, the big cats in England, the disappearance of songbirds also in England, pelicans dying all along the South American coast because of cold waters driving the anchovies away, the reappearance of the Tasmanian Tiger, the mysterious livestock and pet mutilations in the USA and UK - The list could be twenty times as long but the overall pattern of a world that is becoming harsher in its environmental and spiritual ambience is clear.

It seems that an understanding of the more subtle forces at work in the universe is imperative if we are to progress beyond a desire to control and dominate. Science alone will not achieve this but then neither will mysticism, which has a tendency to stand by and look helpless at proceedings. Perhaps something like the geomancy and Feng Shui outlined in this book can do a lot to bridge the gap between earth and spirit, even when the spirit in question causes our hearts to beat a little too fast.

Shadows in the Stream

I was staying in an old English manor when there was an incident of a young boy being quite distraught at apparently seeing a ghost. I asked him later what the ghost looked like. After he told me, I didn't say anything and kept a certain fact to myself: namely, that I had seen exactly the same apparition five years earlier.

The house was haunted in the classical British manner (if you'll pardon the pun) by various entities: the vague form of a woman in nineteenth century dress was often seen, once in two separate rooms on the same night; the crying of a baby heard on the first floor landing, usually in daylight; and even our black dog friend put in an appearance once.

A long time before this I once stayed in a reputedly haunted room, which didn't bother me till I was woken from an early night's sleep sometime after midnight by noises on the first floor landing outside. I lay quietly listening. All the house was silent apart from what was going on outside my door.

It was quite distinctly the sound of people walking round and round the landing.

I couldn't not investigate and, with my heart beating faster, I went to the door and threw it open.

There was nothing there but I could still hear it.

It was the sound of floorboards contracting one-by-one from the cooling of the house, sounding very much like footsteps.

That early experience of a 'ghost' emphasised for me the value of scepticism but, when confronted by other phenomena not so easily explained I found that scepticism had to move into areas not recognised by material science. On seeing the same form the young boy had - a small blonde girl in a Victorian dress - I was driven to seek an explanation of sorts. The answer came through various pages from Theosophists, Eastern thinkers and esoteric literature. These in their own way outlined a profound and ancient science, albeit a science of the inner rather than the outer, but still totally pragmatic in its own way.

A recurring notion, I found, was that each of us has more than one body. The fourth to seventh bodies are beyond the immediate interests of this book, so we are only really concerned with the first three.

This is my understanding of them: The first body is physical and we all know what that is. The second is more subtle, occasionally seen as an aura around us, and in the West is known as the etheric body. This is reputedly the origin of many diseases, before they manifest in the physical body, and where 'energies' such as the black dog entity are likely to get stuck.

The third, though, is where much of the action is, as far as we are concerned: it is known as the astral body.

This third body has several individual characteristics, including: it frequently leaves the physical body on what is known as astral flight, usually when we are sleeping; it is similar in appearance to the physical body; and, after the demise of the physical body it takes about two weeks in order to decay.

Complications arise though when the astral body is 'taken over' by another, usually unknown entity because, instead of decaying, the astral shell is now given a new lease of life. Theosophists refer to this reanimated astral form as a 'shade'. A shade can exist for hundreds of years, looking very much like the original physical body, thus giving rise to reports of a 'ghost'.

Usually a shade is harmless, it just goes about its business, whatever that is, and can even increase the market value of a house. An old English mansion with a ghost is often coveted by Americans as it is deemed to have 'character'. The problem is when the entity occuping the astral form is malevolent and then the haunting definitely loses its quaintness.

The worst case of this I personally ever came across was actually with the little blonde girl who, it will now be appreciated, was not a little blonde girl at all. Her appearance both times was accompanied with a general air of menace. The night that I saw her many of the occupants of the house had nightmares, the most striking of which was about a witch burning everybody in their beds.

This was a complicated case and I'm simplifying it considerably here in order to use it as an example and not get lost in details.

There are two items of background research that are relevant: firstly, that there was a girl murdered by her father at the turn of the century; and, secondly, that the location of the murder was precisely on a black stream.

In this case it was the black stream which provided the malefic 'fuel' for the reanimation of the astral body.

Every case is different but in this one a journey was involved for several miles along the line to a Dragon Heart (or 'power point') where the line converged with others. There a small fire was lit, freeing the stuck energy.

I cannot emphasise enough here the fallacy of thinking that one cure will suit all: in most cases a fire would actually be disastrous in such a place. It was only after much contemplation and consideration, asking with the 'hands on earth' technique that myself and my companion were convinced it was the right thing to do.

So now we have come full circle, back to the subject of when there is something intrinsically wrong with the flow of the earth ch'i itself. The murder by itself would not have caused the problems it did. The additional factor of the black steam, with all its multifarious causes, was needed in order to propagate the destructive ch'i.

Was there a happy ending to the ghost story? Only partially. We're not in the business of fast words and snappy cures here, as that's largely what got us into this environmental mess in the first place, and the line would need considerable more assistance to be in good health again. But the general air of menace in the house was lifted successfully, which was the main point of the exercise, and it can only be hoped that others living alongside the line felt the subtle benefits as well.

One of the important elements in this story was the fact that the body was simply dumped before being found some time later. The ghost of a murder victim is a recurring theme in many countries, the 'spirit' appearing before the living until its corpse is discovered and given a proper burial.

An intelligence is in evidence when it comes to various indigenous cultures burying their dead; there is a sense to it which has parallels of understanding throughout the world. Again, intrinsic to this understanding is the belief that we are each composed of various bodies.

In ancient Egypt they spoke of ka, akh and ba spirits, whereas in early China the belief was simple in that the spirits of the dead stayed in the earth close to their corpses before eventually merging with the yin energies of the earth. A later development had the 'hun' soul moving into an afterlife, with the 'po' soul staying with the earth. The po soul would then be the intermediary between the living and their ancestors, a function given extra longevity through the corpse's burial in fairly yang soil. This explains the Chinese emphasis on the correct siting of graves, with a deliberate, conscious prolonging of activity of the po soul (almost certainly identical to the 'astral body' and perhaps the Egyptian ka spirit). It was only when there was an unhealthy disturbance that the po soul would become an unhealthy influence, a 'ghost'; a fact used by enemies of a lineage as they could effectively destroy the roots of that family by destroying their ancestors' graves. It is

Sacred Angles

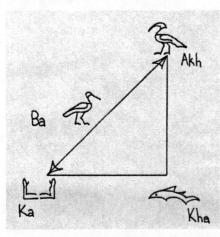

In ancient Egypt the relationship between the physical body and three subtle bodies was depicted as a right-angled triangle.

Drawing by Emma Jones

possible that the European tradition of burying nobility in churches is an echo of an old, similar concept: preserving something of the life-force.

There was the example in an earlier chapter of homes affected by a graveyard on a predominantly yang site. This is not an uncommon situation. Another place I once had to work on in England has a hospital on a very yang site on the crest of a hill, with its accompanying graveyard alongside it. This too is causing a disturbance among the dragon currents for the surrounding area, though the effect is somewhat mitigated in this particular case by the cemetery being to the North of the site; the North and West areas often being favoured for burial in traditional Feng Shui because of their obvious yin qualities.

An appreciation of the complexities inherent in choosing a good burial site should encourage more respect for ancient beliefs in this subject; but, in the absence of any deliberate placement of graves, the very least one can do is only choose yin sites so that the departed really can rest in peace.

Ghost Busting

The complications inherent in the case of a 'haunting' should be obvious at this stage. Not only do we have the tangle of various lines on a site, from which we have to discern those which are relevant, we also have the numerous types of entity that can appear, none of which really subscribe to the classical 'ghost' now that we really look at the subject. There is much more as well far and beyond the scope of this chapter, particularly as we are likely in this work to impinge on the Unknowable as well as the Unknown.

A question to be asked is: to what extent is 'ghost busting' desirable or even relevant? In Britain - generally accepted as the most haunted land in the world - many people live side-by-side with their spectral house-sharers and there is no problem. In Ben Okri's 'The Famished Road', not only is the depiction of a primeval 'memory of roads' in Nigeria remarkable, but also the ways in which spirits and human beings interact on a continual basis. It is to the credit of his writing, in fact, that Okri makes the behaviour of politicians seem more bizarre and unsettling than that of the ghosts!

The presence of the mysterious can, therefore, be a desirable reminder of worlds beyond our own and it is actually the spiritual death of our landscapes, as we have seen, which is at the core of many of our problems.

Ghost busting is only necessary when there is a presence of an energy that is life-threatening or - as in most cases, less dramatically and more subtlely - life-negating. Put simply, this is energy that is in the wrong time at the wrong place. Sometimes though, it is people who are in the wrong place. One of the worst houses I ever had to examine had a spate of murders, sickness and various paranormal phenomena including a poltergeist and self-starting fires. The location

Spirit House, Bangkok

In Thailand special structures are sometimes built in order to house spirits. In this example, it can be seen that the taller yang structure of the office block will benefit from any stray yin energies being drawn into the Spirit House.

Photograph by Sam Hardy

was what I called a Kali Sanctuary, a place solely for the destructive forces of the universe and totally inappropriate for healthy families and businesses which, of course, mostly need the creative part of the natural cycle.

The most common aspect of the more harmful 'hauntings' is an intrusion of the past into the present. In the case of the Kali Sanctuary, the inhabitants were 'buying into' the energies of the place by behaving destructively themselves, but this can occur in much more subtle ways as well. One of the first things a Feng Shui practitioner tends to ask is about the past history of a place, for not only can this give clues as to the dynamics of the site it can also reveal the presence of patterns, behaviour that is likely to be unconsciously repeated by later inhabitants. This was the subject of the book 'The Owl Service' by Alan Garner, ostensibly written for teenagers but with much of interest for older readers. The story reveals how an unconscious willingness of inhabitants is required to keep the fires of the past burning, no matter how destructive.

It is because of this intrusion of the past that a cleansing ritual is normally needed, followed soon after by a party - a house-warming party if the place has just been moved into. This is a way of saying 'goodbye' to the past and welcoming in the present.

There are many ways of cleansing a premises from unwanted influences. Some people use meditation techniques, chanting, singing or prayer. All this and more can be used in conjunction with smudging, one of the most popular methods, a technique acquired from Native American rituals. This involves the burning of a stick of herbs as you move around a site. The principal herb in America is desert sage. Unfortunately the demand for smudge sticks has led to both commercial exploitation, by mass harvesting in the States replacing what was once a sacred, careful gathering, and also to an ignorance of the sheer potency of local herbs. Rather than purchasing a smudge stick from New Age stores, it is better by far to find out what the best plants for cleansing are in your area. In Europe I usually use a combination of sage with rosemary, tying them with twine into one-inch thick bundles about a foot in length then leaving them to dry in a warm place for a few days.

Action:

When you do the smudging ritual be extremely careful. Carry a bowl or plate under the burning herbs, watch out for any escaping sparks and don't leave the stick burning unattended.

Visit all the areas of the house and the smoke will permeate everything for a few hours. You can adapt the ritual however you like, in the way you feel is sacred for you.

Another consideration to all this is the yin/yang balance. Spiritual forces are yin by definition and thrive in dominantly yin houses, hence the classical dark, labyrinthine haunted house. So the simple solution in such cases is to bring in more of the yang - usually through light and noise. An Oxford newspaper reported the story of a man who had unwittingly moved into a house plagued with paranormal phenomena. His friends and colleagues, for a joke, turned up in a van made to look like the one from the American 'Ghostbusters' movies. Dressed in similarly outrageous gear, they charged around the house, spraying it with confetti and party toys. To everyone's astonishment it worked as their friend was never bothered again by the ghost. Unwittingly they had done an extremely good cleansing ritual, bringing in the yang with bright colours, loud noises - and humour. Schools are also rarely haunted as long as the children are present, but at night - or in the holidays if it's a boarding school - the sudden switch from extreme yang to yin can provoke quite a number of disturbances.

Salt has a reputation for being useful in 'spooky' situations. There is a possible scientific explanation in that salt destroys microbiological organisms (important exceptions being cholera and the MRSA superbug). The esoteric explanation for salt's effectiveness is that it has the ability to absorb excessive yin energies, hence the classical 'magic circle', which could tie in with the fact that it dehydrates cells, sucking the water out via osmosis (water being yin). Romans would sprinkle salt on fields after battles in order to encourage the spirits to rest. In Japan there is a traditional 'laying of salt' ritual known as kiyomeru, still enacted in rural areas today. So, if you find yourself in a psychically volatile situation, you may want to keep a bowl of salt nearby, such as by your bed.

A combination of a cleansing ritual and an emphasis on the yang is usually enough to deal with any intrusion of the past or unwanted spiritual forces, whether it's just the bad moods from previous inhabitants still hanging around or something more disturbing. Usually no more action is required but in some cases, as we have already seen, there are complications, which is when further detective work is required.

It is to be hoped that this chapter will help encourage a respect for forces we do not necessarily understand but that we can still work with: and also an awareness of the richness and complexity of some cases. It should be clear by now that every case is unique and requires much research and thought before any action is taken beyond that of simple cleansing. One of the best case histories with this in mind is recounted in 'Testimony' by Mark Chadbourn, about a severely haunted house in Wales. It is an excellent disaster story, with many false turnings along the way, involving dowsers, psychics and priests; and the ultimate resolution being as astonishing as the journey which took them there.

I am often asked when abroad why Britain has so many ghosts. I have no answer to that, though I often wonder if they're not a sort of 'psychic fallout' from the manipulation of the earth currents, through the Bronze Age standing stones and other monuments from the past. But another aspect is that some of the ghosts are indicative of Britain's rich heritage - not a stable, 'permanent' phenomenon as some would have us believe but an identity that has always undergone change through the continual fusion of various cultures.

The problem nowadays though is not so much with things that go bump in the night, but rather the creation of a totally dead landscape, one without colour, without character - totally lacking in spirit. This is more chilling than anything described in these last pages and it is a situation that is worldwide.

On to the next chapter.

Related Reading

The Astral Body	A. E. Powell	(Theosophical)
The Beast of Exmoor	Trevor Beer	(Countryside)
Daimonic Reality	Patrick Harpur	(Penguin)
The Famished Road	Ben Okri	(Vintage)
The Holographic Universe	Michael Talbot	(Harper Collins)
The Owl Service	Alan Garner	(Collins)
Psychology of the Esoteric	Osho	(Rebel)
Testimony	Mark Chadbourn	(Vista)

Chapter 8

The Poisoned Dragon

The West has become a world of things, not people.

Cheikh Hamidou Kane,
Senegalese novelist

Consciousness of the Land

In 1992 a war was fought at Twyford Down near Winchester in England, a site considered by some to have actually been Camelot and designated officially an Area of Outstanding Beauty. The war was fought between those wishing to build an extra bit of road, thus reducing the London-Southampton journey by five minutes, and those for whom the site was either sacred or simply beautiful.

Naturally - or unnaturally, rather - the former won, but not without some cost. Not only was the road development delayed by two months due to the presence of the protesters, two workmen had fatal heart attacks and a security guard collapsed and died. There was talk of a curse, not unlike those associated with the ransacking of the pyramids and various ancient tombs. Eighteen bodies had been found, some over seven feet tall, amidst an assortment of burial mounds and Celtic field systems. People had been living and dying there for over three thousand years. Now it's a motorway.

Of course, this is not an unusual story. All around the world there are and have been similar anecdotes of short-term interests triumphing over aesthetics and sanctity. Wherever you are now there will certainly be an example nearby.

An economist with environmentalist leanings once said to me, 'The only real problem is over-population. Once that is sorted, everything else will be sorted.' This is partially true, but only partially. It is easy to imagine that if there were less people there would be less pollution, fewer social problems and the systematic destruction of our planet would cease. On the other hand, even a casual glance at history reveals that most peoples around the world in the past were quite intent at doing nasty things to their neighbours and to themselves, no matter how few were living in any particular area. We are simply at the point now where such behaviour is more likely to lead to global annihilation.

Sometimes you can make an immediate and direct connection with consciousness and the environment. The Japanese have been facing a serious problem with deforestation due to the amount of timber required for the popular Manga comic books. While some of the Manga are excellent, many are rubbish - and perverse rubbish at that, by most standards. Littering subway trains in Tokyo sometimes are Manga, abandoned after one read, depicting subjects such as businessmen cheerfully gang-raping a schoolgirl. A more direct connection between the poverty of our consciousness and the devastation of our landscape could not be made. Yet this is not especially the Japanese. It is all of us.

The chief concern in this book is not to attempt to address a myriad social and economic ills but to focus on one over-riding theme: putting the spirit back in the land. This is where ecology falls short for it deals only with the physical problems in the environment. The source of the dragon's poison is much deeper than that.

We looked earlier in Chapter Three how a green activist can be doing all the right things for the wrong reasons, with a price to pay for that inconsistency eventually. Yet you can take it for granted that there is no condoning of ecological atrocities in these pages. For instance, when looking at ideas for altering the presence of factories or cars in the landscape, there will be an unspoken assumption that dealing with pollution is absolutely vital as well. It is just that here we are concentrating on the invisible factors and it is in this role that disciplines such as Feng Shui flourish: by bridging the gap between earth and spirit.

My own vested interest in all this is that I like the modern world so much that I would like it to stick around a bit longer. Acquaintances are often slightly perturbed that friends and I who work with green issues sometimes drive sports cars. I love driving. I also enjoy being able to wake up the next day in a totally different country, I'm fascinated by space exploration and by science in general, I like television. It's an exciting time, a time when new discoveries are being made every day; and history shows that technology never goes backward, unless in sudden mythical and cleansing Atlantean cataclysms.

Let's hope it doesn't come to that for this is also a time when national boundaries are breaking down and we are witnessing the rather difficult birth of a truly global community. But how successful can this birth be if we do not know who we are, if we do not know the Earth which is mother of us all?

Some people do choose to return to a more primitive lifestyle but most of us will not want to be without plumbing, electricity, telephones, cars, television etc. My father, who worked with environmental issues in South Africa, once had a meeting with San (bushmen). Some of them informed him that while other people wanted them to retain their basic lifestyle, they in fact wished to have cars and other mod cons. This is a common situation: while those of us who lead complex, technological lives wish to retain them, we paradoxically wish others to continue living 'naturally', as a sort of token gesture to the Earth. Another example would be the Amish in Pennsylvania having to put up with hordes of tourists every year because they choose to live simply. We won't live like that but we'll go and watch others doing so, preferably on TV.

Yet even television has brought about some of the greatest changes in mankind, albeit subtlely and sometimes even by accident. Apparently 'Baywatch', of all things, caused a near feminist revolt in one Middle Eastern country when women realised they could wear bikinis, be heroic, have fun, be themselves. 'Baywatch' got banned in that country as a result. In South Africa I witnessed, in a house where racial equality was being discussed fervently amongst the adults, a young child watching Star Trek in another room. Zero discrimination was already a reality in his mind as it was in the minds of that show's creators.

This subtle, paradoxical influence of technology has brought many gifts to the world. It in itself is not necessarily harmful but the intelligence behind it can be, which is something of a truism but is worth saying nonetheless. Viktor Schauberger, whose work we're going to examine briefly next, didn't see pollution as a problem but more as the symptom of a problem - which was the result of man's consciousness leading to a technology that was unnatural.

It is worth bearing in mind also that the greatest threat to life on this planet through pollution came about two billion years ago. This was when lazy microbes decided to get a free lunch by synthesising energy directly from the sun. The substance used to bring this about was chlorophyll and the deadly waste product was oxygen. It could have wiped out the entire planet but that didn't happen. Instead it gave birth to a new type of life that utilised the oxygen for energy, with carbon dioxide as a waste product, thus enabling evolution to progress beyond the microbe stage and start producing larger life-forms.

A recent step in evolution is a life-form that can actually consciously decide what is harmful and what is not - and that requires responsibility. Living naturally is partly a question of attitude, but more than that it is a question of who and what we are in relation to the world around us.

Earth's Blood

There is an Australian Aboriginal belief that koala bears have a secret weapon, which is to induce drought if their habitat is threatened. This does not seem so far-fetched when looking at the simultaneity of the destruction of the Australian rainforest and the onslaught of severe droughts in latter years. It seems even more feasible when considering the direct connection between consciousness and the environment, and it also relates to the evidence offered by an Austrian called Viktor Schauberger.

Schauberger's appalling treatment by scientific, business and political establishments parallels that of other maverick geniuses, such as Wilhem Reich, and consequently his work is relegated to that of 'alternative' (of which the sub-text is: 'not worth taking seriously'). He died in 1958 but his contribution to an understanding of the natural environment is impressive; and many of those with an interest in subjects like Feng Shui and ecology are benefiting from studying his work. Slowly, like the initial flow from the sources of water that he spent a lifetime studying, his legacy is starting to take effect.

One of the many interesting facts of Schauberger's life was that he learnt directly from Nature and from the traditions of his area and family, who had been foresters for generations. Olof Alexandersson tells of an early experience of Schauberger's that was to prove influential, when he was in a remote part of the forest with hunters who were puzzled at the unprecedented drying up of a spring. They rebuilt the old stone structure that had previously covered the spring and the water consequently returned. Later an explanation could be provided through an understanding of water reaching its maximum density at the 'anomaly point' of +4 degrees Celsius, which the exposure to sunlight had prevented; but the point here is that the lesson was received directly from Nature and not a laboratory, which typifies Schauberger's approach and his consequent discord with science.

The parallel between some of Schauberger's insights about forests and the Australian situation mentioned above, is that Schauberger saw a forest as being an energetic power centre for the environment surrounding it, with flowing water as the acting medium. In practical terms this is shown in the way water does not complete its full cycle in the absence of a forest as invaluable trace elements cannot be brought to the surface.

This has immediate implications in terms of the Chinese Five Elements. Britain has gone through several stages of deforestation, but one of the most recent surges of it was in the sixteenth century when England was frantically building ships in order to establish its Empire. Anyone going to see the famous Nottingham Forest today is going to be disappointed as there is nowhere left for Robin Hood to hide. Another place in the UK that has undergone extreme deforestation is Cornwall. The presence of the sea is inescapable in that county, which is why it is so popular with tourists (though they're not so fond of the regular bouts of rain) and indisputably one of its overwhelmingly beautiful characteristics.

The problem here is that the absence of trees not only contains the environmental implications as forewarned by Schauberger, it also makes Water the dominant element without the next one in the creative cycle: that is, Wood. I often encourage clients in Cornwall to bring in more of the Wood element into their homes, explaining that otherwise their Fire is likely to keep getting doused - which usually manifests through a lack of ascension in life, great plans and enthusiasm which don't come to fruition. There are a lot of frustrated people in that county. Of course, the ideal is to plant more trees. I must add here that I am not advocating this for every area with a strong presence of the Water element. Every place is different. Portugal, for instance, also very connected to the sea, has a totally different dynamic - there one can perceive the dominant elements as being Earth (the yellow sand), Metal (the rounded hills and white houses) and Water (the sea).

Much of Schauberger's interest was in the movement of water, an understanding he used to transport timber with extreme cost efficiency. 'First understand Nature, then copy it,' was his maxim. This appreciation of natural movement led also to his denunciation of conventional water management, the latter demonstrated so disturbingly by the straightening of the Rhine. What were once crystal-clear waters are now simply the sludge of a dying river. The need for gentle, meandering curves in Nature is something that would be insisted upon also by a Feng Shui practitioner.

Another concern of Schauberger's was the detrimental effect that iron machinery was having on the landscape, something that first came to his attention when he noticed that Turkish farms in Bulgaria were still using wooden ploughs in the 1930's and were experiencing superior harvests. His observations showed that water disappeared rapidly from fields that had been tilled by iron ploughs, due to the breaking of magnetic fields by the iron, leading to electrolysis - the splitting of water into hydrogen and oxygen. I came across a variation on the same theme when following a dragon line that crossed railway tracks.

The first thing I noticed when still quite some distance from the tracks, was that there was a tension on the line itself every time a train approached - like somebody expecting to be hit and bracing themselves. When the train disappeared, the line relaxed. What was even more interesting was the effect the tracks had on the immediate area surrounding them. The ch'i of the line would fragment - resulting in an outpouring of ch'i on both sides of the tracks. Nature was therefore extremely abundant in the immediate vicinity of the railway, albeit chaotic, but the main price to pay came further away - the line had 'spent' it's ch'i by the tracks, which meant it was severely depleted a mile further on in the direction of its flow. The irony is that, in terms of real estate, the properties by the tracks were rated low in value but in actual fact were in a much healthier state than the more expensive houses a mile and further away. I knew people on both 'sides of the tracks' and the poorer were definitely the happier!

A solution to this state of affairs is not clear. Schauberger developed a copper spiral plough, the copper not having the same effect as the iron and the spiral imitating the burrowing movements of a mole. In Indian villages water and drink are often kept in copper barrels because the quality of the sustenance is improved and perpetuated.

Where this leaves us in relation to railway tracks I have no idea. The first step is simply to acknowledge that we have a problem.

The Nature of Journeys

On a last-minute flight to Maastricht one year, the cabin lights of the small plane I was on were turned off as per usual, when we left the airport at Stanstead. The plane was of the old propeller-driven type, which I've always loved, and the ascent was much slower. This gave time to look down at the night scene below us in a leisurely fashion.

I was struck by the beauty of the traffic on the busy roads beneath us. From afar it all looked so peaceful. It also reminded me of a bloodstream in a human body: the stream of white headlights could be the blood cells moving towards the lungs, the red tail-lights oxygenated blood moving away and the occasional blue flashing lights of emergency services the white blood cells moving rapidly to deal with problems.

Back on ground level, of course, we have created hell on Earth. The amount of deaths caused by the automobile every year are so high that Heathcote Williams in his appropriately-named book 'Autogeddon' calls it 'the Third World War that nobody bothered to declare'. Horror stories abound and we have all experienced directly - or know people who have - extremely disturbing events on the road. We voluntarily subject ourselves to the possibility of dying at any moment if one little thing goes wrong, a source of tension that our ancestors never had to put up with for such extended periods of time. As if to emphasise this, Feng Shui relates the car to a tiger: moving close to the ground, powerful, forceful and dangerous. Yet we still choose to drive.

If we could sum up the need for the car in one word it would probably be 'Freedom' - or, more precisely, a sense of power to grant that freedom - a notion that early advertisers for the car were quick to cash in on. There is the obvious connection with a need to visit places that might otherwise be out of reach. There is also more simply the freedom in little things, such as going to do the shopping when one wants or to visit a friend. A speedster - whether a racing car driver or a joy-rider - can experience freedom briefly through emotional catharsis. Even the transport of goods can be seen as an aspect of freedom - the freedom to have what we want when we want it. The really extreme and therefore most damaging aspects of this seem two-fold: one is the urge to escape - what are we escaping from? - and the other is the sense of 'desperately seeking something'.

The latter point is easily addressed: we are seeking sex. Eliot Cowan (cf Chapter Three) makes the observation that pictures of the female breast are omnipresent in the car industry - visible in promotion material, garages, you name it - and he sees our aberrant behaviour on the roads as the manifestation of an Earth imbalance in relation to the Five Elements, that we are unconsciously seeking the breast of our Earth Mother. "It is absolutely true that a car is symbolic of a man's sexual organ," said a Scottish comedian in his shiny sports car before realising that the ignition wouldn't work.

The comedian was making a wry comment on male egos but women are not exempt either. A friend of mine has successfully combined a business career with environmental concerns. In other words, she has succeeded in a male-dominated field yet still managed to stay in tune with the 'Earth Mother'. And with her long black hair and mauve contours of the car, she looks good. Even here the car acts as a yang symbol, one that says 'I have succeeded'.

None of this is intended to disparage an enjoyment of cars, merely to point out some of the psychological 'drives' lurking in the background. It is to be hoped that this way, when our hidden imperatives become clear, we are actually more free to appreciate driving for itself.

The urge to escape is the other sign of an imbalance with our driving habits and this takes us full circle right back to the underlying concerns surrounding our immediate habitats, because the implication is that we have created homes that we do not find truly nourishing. The joke is that it is partly the car we have to blame for it. Here are some of the costs of having the car a strong presence in our lives:

- Suburbs have arisen only because of the car. They have been created because of the easy access that cars provided. These 'new villages' are now absolutely car dependent and generally have no deep connection with the spirit of place.

- Town centres have died - or at least become dormant. For older towns anywhere in the world the centre was not accidental - it functioned as the omphalos, the sacred centre and heart of the town and an essential connection with the Dragon Heart.

- Main streets, once the chief artery of towns, are now almost inaccessible due to the traffic. A place where people once mingled, met and talked to each other is now hostile to personal contact. This has also destroyed the front door for many homes, forcing people to use only the rear entrance. This causes complications in Feng Shui through a new, unnatural duality and imbalance in the home.

- Noise and chemical pollution requires us to use various types of shields around our homes, usually barriers of thick vegetation and double-glazing. Houses have become fortresses.

Putting all this plus other factors together we can summarise extreme (but also extremely common) cases like this: *We've created homes we want to escape from, through using roads we can't stand, in order to trash out the places we visit.*

The first part of that statement refers to the need to enhance our life-style in a deep and meaningful way and that is ultimately the task of Feng Shui: to add meaning to our lives, to deepen our connection with the Earth and the cosmos.

Part and parcel of that is our propensity to know ourselves, whether through the Five Element system or otherwise.

The remainder of the statement, concerning our roads and where we visit, I'd like to look at now.

Some of the best architects in the world are well aware of the inner as well as the outer discord brought about by the car, and the books on architecture listed at the end of this chapter are representative. I don't wish to go over old ground (except literally, as we'll see) so I'm going to concentrate on areas that might otherwise be missed.

The nature of the average journey has changed intrinsically in even more than the obvious ways. In ancient times temples and centres of commerce were often at the same locations. This meant that, when going somewhere to trade, it was a sacred journey, accomplished by following the dragon paths. The implication is that inevitably more would be gained from such a journey than a bag of vegetables. The modern day equivalent is the supermarket, devoid of anything other than commerce, and sucking the ch'i away from any natural centres. Even here though miracles can happen. Many stores in Britain have been featured in the media because of particular checkout counters where the girl working there invariably gets pregnant. A bit of observation in your nearest supermarket might reveal also a till where something always goes wrong, eg there is only one person ahead of you in

Echoing Nature

A yin valley road in North Devon. You can't always use it in the winter months but it's always beautiful.

the queue but something they've bought won't scan and you are delayed considerably. In both cases - the pregnancy counter and the 'cursed' counter - there is a line going through; which is actually inevitable, if you think about the sheer length covered by a row of checkouts. If the lung mei in a supermarket could be encouraged and enhanced, then we would be talking real business on all levels. In a positive sense, it is noticeable that in the more remote areas a supermarket may be the only place open at certain times, its activities, lights and colours the only vibrant source of ch'i for miles around. Local garages also often fulfil this function.

Old roads tended to follow dragon paths, as we have seen. This was particularly true in that in places such as Europe the journeys in the valleys were too hazardous for horse-drawn vehicles, prone as they were to flooding and excessive mud. The higher ground was therefore preferred, which meant that journeys were in tune with the more yang lines; now that technology has enabled us to drive with more safety on lower ground, we are often following lines that are more yin. These have their own beauty that can be enhanced as well. Some of the best valley roads echo the course of rivers. No matter how busy these roads become, the gentle curves and the occasional glimpses of water, with the sun glistening on its surface, guarantee a life-enhancing journey. Nevertheless, I have come across cases of depression and melancholy in people who continually travel along valley routes and it has been necessary to counter their effect by following higher roads on occasion.

The Chinese saying is that 'demons fly in straight lines' and it is the tyranny of the straight line that we seek to avoid. In houses people sometimes use wind-chimes or mobiles to break up the 'killing ch'i' of a corridor. On a long straight road we are more aware of sheer tedium than anything else. Bill Bryson in 'The Lost Continent' reveals much of the pros and cons of the contemporary landscape through months of travelling on the American roads. One of his observations is how large advertising billboards by the sides of roads did a lot to break the monotony. I also find the long lines of poplars in Italy and France performing a similar function, their leaves shimmering and turning in the wind, like giant mobiles. One of the suggestions made by architects has been to raise sidewalks in cities, even by a few inches, but in a random fashion so that this enables pedestrians to have a delineated territory and also softens the straight lines of the streets. As mentioned in the first chapter, architects in Beijing did the same thing centuries ago.

There are other ways that roads could be enhanced:

- Next to the M5 in England there was the life-size model of a camel for many years, which some enterprising soul placed there, consequently breaking the monotony of that stretch of road through the sheer unexpectedness of the sight. Also, prisoners in North England had to plant flowers by the side of a road, which they did. When Spring arrived the blooms spelt out a number of swear-words in giant letters - the mens' creativity ensured that nobody would forget that spot in a hurry. Similar - but perhaps less provocative! - methods should be encouraged.

- It has been shown that drivers who have to commute regularly experience improved moods if their route takes them through stretches of forest.

- In Switzerland some of the factories are painted in bright colours so that instead of meeting an eye-sore when you turn the corner you are pleasantly surprised.

- Being stuck behind a lorry for miles and miles would be a totally different experience if the back of the lorry were something worth looking at. You can notice this for yourself the next few times you're in this situation, because that which is in front of you is your Red Phoenix (cf Chapter Two) and when that is blocked in our lives feelings of frustration inevitably build up. Transport companies could utilise this space for enhancing the environment and excellent advertising far superior to the cheap slogans normally seen on the backs of trucks.

Actions:

On a more personal scale, there are ways in which you can take responsibility for your journey.

Action 1:

Work on the interior environment of your car. Keep it tidy and clean, have a cloth handy on which you can sprinkle natural oils, such as lavender for relaxing and citrus for alertness, and install an ioniser. Clean your windows - they are the eyes of the vehicle and dirty windows have been linked to increased stress on the roads. Expand your horizons by listening to music and radio stations you wouldn't normally. You may wish to attach an earthing cable to the rear of your car to release the static that builds up on the chassis. This is particularly important in built-up areas where you are passing to and fro under electrical pylons on a regular basis. You also have a right to drive slowly and carefully: if tailgators are a problem, stick a deflective symbol on the back of your car - I used a pair of cheerfully menacing cartoon eyes and have had no problems since with impatient drivers behind as they all pull back instinctively.

Action 2:

Vary your journey. Don't always take the quickest route but allow extra time to explore other possibilities. By far the best way in which to accomplish this is to start following the dragon lines that you may have worked out previously. Even if you return eventually to the faster route, your knowledge of and connection to the area will be incalculably deepened. You are also likely to become aware of accident black spots, which are often where roads cross black streams, and can therefore be more careful when traversing those places. It also helps to have a compass on the dashboard - this enables you to be more aware of the directions you move in, with any effect they may be having on you (cf Chapter Two), and also helps when you 'go rogue' by following dragon lines on smaller roads instead of the usual routes.

Action 3:

As an extension to the last points, be aware of the yin and yang of your journeys. If you are constantly travelling on high ground, the excessive yang may manifest as stress and a lack of enjoyment/appreciation of your journey. Balance this with more yin routes, such as alongside rivers and valley roads. (Chill out!) Contrariwise, if your journeys are predominantly yin - dark wooded areas, low ground etc. - then a subtle melancholy and depressiveness may be finding its way into your psyche. To gain confidence and exhilaration, seek the high ground. In both cases, you will probably need to allow extra time for your journeys but it will be worth it.

A Home Is Not A Castle

In Amsterdam the Dutch have experimented successfully with woonerf streets or 'Home Zones', areas where the car is almost completely barred and the emphasis is on creating soft, healthy environments - for people. This is definitely one way to do it but there are places, particularly rural, that rely on the car to bring much-needed ch'i to the area, so what can you do if you are in close proximity to a road? Well, you can enhance the nature of others' journeys even when you're not partaking in them yourself, something that should still bring immediate benefits to you as part of a community assailed by traffic:

Action:

If you yourself have a house or business uncomfortably close to a road, instead of becoming just another blank spot to pass by unnoticed, challenge that by enhancing the exterior of your building. Perhaps you want to use brightly coloured windmills or beautiful or funny statues. Use your imagination! And if you can 'tune in' the decor with the lung mei of the site, as described in Chapter Five, even better. If you feel in tune with the lung mei, chalk something representative - a symbol or picture - on any part of the road where a dragon line crosses; or place appropriate statues adjacent to the road. Don't be another anonymity for people to pass by in a hurry - stand out! Another suggestion for the larger continents - if you have the time and energy - is to establish your own local radio station, making it varied and interesting, something by which people in your area and those passing through can have their lives enhanced.

These methods will help in enhancing the ch'i of an area and hopefully slow down the relentless killing ch'i of the road, though it is obviously essential to deal with the issue on a purely practical level. This applies to the building itself as much as it does to traffic calming:

- Plenty of vegetation between the site and the road will cut down the noise pollution considerably. As well as trees, this includes climber plants such as Virginia Creeper. Irregular surfaces absorb sound much more efficiently than regular, smooth ones, particularly if those surfaces are inclined rather than vertical.

- A ha-ha - a hidden dip that conceals a hedge, fence or wall - is very effective. It also creates a boundary that is not offensive to the eye.

- Ionisation - from an indoor fountain or ioniser - and VOC-absorbing plants (see below) will improve the air quality inside the house. Double-glazing, of course, helps the sound quality.

- Garages are usually best on the right (White Tiger) side of a building.

Quo Vadis?

Roman-like, we tend to prefer to go straight to our destinations; but once we are there, what is their nature, their quality? Those which are functional yet require enhancement such as our workplaces are self-evident, but there is a problem with beauty-spots as well. In Venice I came across an environmental pressure group pointing out the hypocrisy inherent in people making their own habitats so repellent that they needed to come to Venice in order to recuperate. Their concern was the sheer amount of damage that city was experiencing due to its onslaught of visitors. Even as we make our first tentative moves into Space, we seem intent on continuing our path of destruction - orbital junk debris became a serious problem decades ago.

Bad Journey

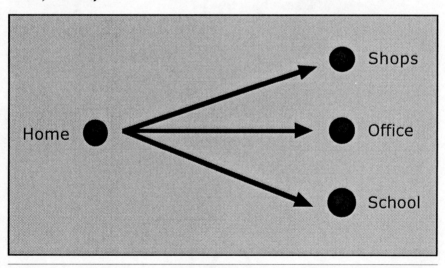

That tourism is presently vital to the economics of many regions is clear. Mallorca was close to Third World status before being revitalised by the tourist industry. African countries recognise that people visit often to see the wildlife, so

Good Journey

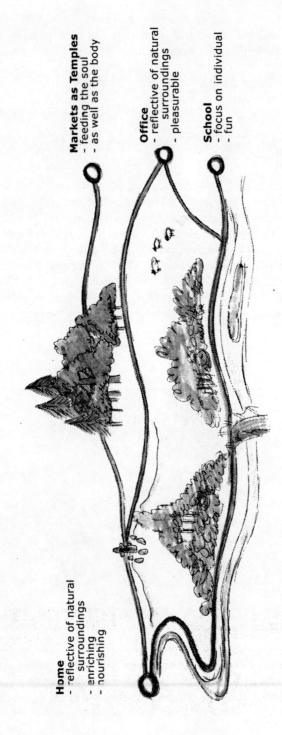

Home
- reflective of natural surroundings
- enriching
- nourishing

Markets as Temples
- feeding the soul
- as well as the body

Office
- reflective of natural surroundings
- pleasurable

School
- focus on individual
- fun

A slow, sensual drive is usually preferable to one where the driver arrives with a sense of desperation. By deepening the experience of the journey our lives can be considerably enhanced, something achieved through less linear routes and an emphasis on quality rather than frequency.

Drawing by Hilary Johnson

wildlife preservation becomes translated into a language that all politicians understand: money.

It is the superficiality of tourism that is in essence the most destructive element, one offshoot of which is the weekend cottage syndrome where city-dwellers buy up the properties in the countryside for an occasional retreat, not a practice likely to encourage deep respect for the land.

I was intrigued with the case of a seaside town in England that proves very popular with tourists. On the surface it's easy to see why. It's thought of as 'old and quaint' - though in reality it is only three hundred years old, which is significantly young in earth energy terms - and has many beautiful vistas over the sea. Yet there is something wrong, a fact of which local people are often aware. Nobody can put their finger on it and define exactly what it is but the feeling is tangible enough to force some shopkeepers to move their premises twenty miles away and for potential traders to drive to the next, not so quaint, town.

I cannot claim to know what the cause of this imbalance is - particularly as I avoid the place as much as possible. The sheer youth of the town I find suspect and the fact that it was built primarily as a trading post in the slave trade era, but the one thing I can vouch for is the effect of a quarry nearby.

Quarries vary a lot as to the amount of devastation they cause to the energy of an area. Some create extreme havoc in the dragon lines and others are less damaging, but there is one factor that I find common to lines passing through quarries: the sense of something having been taken from the Earth with nothing being given back, not even a 'thank you'. In this way some black streams are born. Occasionally quarries have been filled with water, turned into lakes, and when this is appropriate to the energy of that place there is no problem because something has in fact been given back to the land. At other times this doesn't work at all, even lowering the water table of the area and incurring the wrath of farmers who feel powerless against the PR machine of industries that effortlessly rape their landscape.

In the case of the seaside town, the effect was more subtle than this but was definitely one of the contributing factors to the town's malaise. Yet superficially there was no problem. I find this indicative of the tourist industry in general, that it goes by appearances, hoping for a quick-buck glimpse of paradise as 'it's certainly not in evidence back home'.

And so we return to our main theme: it is not the journeys we take that are the issue, it is their nature. It is to be hoped that by enhancing our journeys - including our source and destinations - thus deepening our contact with the Earth, fewer journeys will need to be made. This is important, because unless our deeper needs to travel are addressed, even working entirely at home through the internet and other means is not going to be fulfilling.

Fun With Colour

One way to enhance the relationship between a car and its surroundings is through knowledge of the dominant elements in an environment to choose the appropriate colour for a car. (See Chapter Three regarding the Element cycles.)

The car colours in each group below are listed in order of:

1. Gaining from the environment

2. Merging with the environment

3. Giving to the environment.

Environment	Dominant Colour/Element	Car Colour (Element)
Desert	Yellow/Earth	1 White (Metal) 2 Yellow (Earth) 3 Red (Fire)
Seascape	Blue/Water	1 Green (Wood) 2 Blue/black (Water) 3 White (Metal)
Woods/ green fields	Green/Wood	1 Red (Fire) 2 Green (Wood) 3 Blue/black (Water)

Also, if you have a colour that seems inappropriate, then you can remedy that by using the Creative Cycle. For example, if you have a yellow (Earth) car in a predominantly Wood environment, then why not add some dashes of red (Fire)? The Wood environment will then feed the Fire on your car, which will then nourish the Earth.

Don't take all this too seriously - it can be a lot of fun! - and don't be greedy. Maybe your business will thrive more by giving to the environment rather than taking from it, as I found with my Feng Shui business.

Strange Flowers

Driving along many roads these days one can observe the proliferation of aerials, microwave towers and satellite dishes virtually everywhere. The subject of electromagnetic pollution is a contentious one, with the usual predictable scenario: maverick researchers campaigning for a recognition of the inherent dangers of the new problem and numerous vested interests insisting that there isn't a problem. One person I know had to leave a place rather rapidly after he alleged that a radar beam from a military station swept over an area which coincided with a high rate of breast cancer.

Electromagnetic pollution falls somewhere between that of the tangible and the invisible. There is already plenty of literature to support any investigation into the effects of this new phenomenon, but because of its evasive nature it is worth addressing some issues here that may otherwise be missed, particularly the ways in which the lung mei may be effected.

Not only in the new upsurge of telecommunications aerials but also in the long-since established presence of radio masts, there is a recurring factor in where

Like Attracts Like

The interesting thing here is not so much the phone mast cunningly disguised as a tree, but the fact that the trees were already twisting their branches in response to another influence. Stress - geopathic or something else - existed here long before the mast arrived.

they are positioned: on the greatest vantage points, normally the crests of hills. This means that they are often precisely on Dragon Pulses or similar power points.

Now imagine what these signals might mean symbolically. Pretend you don't know what those aerials are and look at them with a fresh eye.

You are likely to get something quite different from me, but my perception of them is that they are like anthers: the male pollen-generating organs of a flower. This fits with them being usually in very yang locations.

If we take this as a working hypothesis, two aspects emerge: one, the aerials can be seen as a natural flowering from the Earth, brought about through us - and we are part of the Earth no matter how much we try not to be. Two, the type of 'pollen' or signal becomes significant.

Looking closer and more critically at the first observation, if an aerial or mast could be assigned one of the Five Elements, it would probably be Fire: because of the sharp point and because of the fact that it utilises the electromagnetic spectrum - and electricity is of the Fire element as we shall see in the next section. Some of the new digital systems 'flash' bursts of the spectrum at 217 times a second, which means the body is being subjected to excess Fire at that rate. Overall, it is calculated that the increase in the amount of radiation we are bathing in, compared to our ancestors, is hundreds of millions of times. That is a lot of Fire. Looking at Fire imbalance, as we did in Chapter Three, as an association exercise I would come up with words like 'heart burn, heart break, stress, isolation, loneliness...'. This is ironic, considering the point of mobile phones is to enhance communication.

The second point, that of the type of signal or 'pollen' transmitted, is also important. An average mobile phone conversation seems to go like this: "Yes, I'm on the train...Yes, I'll be back the usual time...No, I don't want any peas with the dinner...Oh bzzzshcwzzz we're bzzzshcwzzz into bzzzshcwzzz a tunnel bzzzshcwzzz ..." The average radio broadcast is not much better. A good radio station will make a huge difference, as anyone who spends a lot of time on the roads can testify. Trying to avoid too much judgement - we saw earlier with television how even casual communication assists in breaking boundaries - it is apparent that the quality of the message is an issue. Otherwise the messenger is responsible for transmitting a different kind of pollution: a toxin of unconsciousness. Interestingly, Japanese teenagers reacted early on to the proliferation ot conversational noise by making it 'cool' to transmit text messages via their phones, thus keeping it short and simple.

It will be appreciated that this is all very new ground. Some researchers have touched on this but the actual interaction of microwave signals etc with the lung mei we have hardly begun to understand yet. I know of one case where a radio mast is on a power point and is owned by the military. Practically in the next field an annual re-enactment of a historic battle is fought with great gusto. The overall effect on the relevant line is a constant reinforcement of discord.

But this is one case and I wouldn't give a blanket statement that aerials, whether military or civilian, are necessarily disharmonious with the Earth at all.

To emphasise this point, there is a good example of a positive influence in a remote area of Cornwall.

Goonhilly is billed as 'The Largest Satellite Station in the World' and is owned by British Telecom. The satellite dishes are visible from miles away on an area that would simply otherwise be flat moorland. Because of the beauty of the area and the presence of standing stones and tumuli nearby, it is unlikely that anybody would get permission to build anything even slightly similar to the station nowadays. Yet not only are the dishes oddly beautiful in themselves, breaking the monotony of the land, but they are also in keeping with the Five Elements: their material and shape designates them as being of the Metal element, in harmony with the preceding Earth element (as denoted by the flat landscape).

Goonhilly Down, Cornwall

A satellite dish and standing stone in close proximity to each other, as if to illustrate a way forward through a meeting of scientific and mystical forces.

There was a hidden problem though. One of the lines meeting at the large standing stone right by the station also passed through one of the dishes. When examining this area, I realised there was an imbalance but it took some time to work out what it was. Touching the line between the stone and the dish, it felt energised, actually enjoying the presence of the equipment. On the other side of the stone though, the line was depleted. An imbalance had been created due to the extra 'juice' on the dish's side of the line. Walking along the neglected side - which felt 'low in energy', melancholic - I came to two tumuli, both of which were overgrown and unappealing. Whatever the original function of tumuli, I find they tend to act as regenerators on lines - but not in this case. They needed a bit of help, accomplished here by leaving a quartz crystal in the middle of one - and also through a bit of extra attention by encouraging people to walk on the path between the stone and the tumuli.

An intuitive approach is applicable in other cases as well. Wind farms, for example, may be ecologically sound but their symbolic placement is not always so harmonious. As with satellite dishes and aerials, they appear to add something in quality to some environments and take it away in others.

Action

For undesirable aerials or masts near your home or school, use the Feng Shui mirror technique. Any mirror will do but round or octagonal are usually preferred or, if you wish, a concave one to 'reverse' the image or convex to diminish it. The mirror doesn't have to be large. Even an unwanted CD does the trick. Place the mirror on the outside of your building, aiming it directly at the mast. This will throw back any offending ch'i. While this does not diminish the electromagnetic pollution it could balance things in your favour so that, for instance, the next you know, the company is relocating the aerial to somewhere more appropriate.

Alien Fire

Invisible but very present, the effects of electromagnetic fields are only just beginning to be understood.

Our Martian Homes

Fire In The Home

While there is, quite rightly, a lot of concern about electrical pylons people are generally unaware that they have invited the devil into their homes. Using a field meter, levels of electromagnetic radiation are often revealed to be higher in an average bedroom than they are outside when only fifty metres from a pylon. A lot of attention has been brought to this fact in recent years but dealing with it is not always straightforward. The Germans, ahead of everyone once again with their pragmatism, invented the demand switch (Netzfreischalter) - a device that senses when electricity is not required in the bedroom and cuts the supply till needed again. This helps immensely but there is a problem in that it doesn't necessarily take care of any sources of electromagnetic stress coming from elsewhere in the building, such as from lights on the ceiling of a room below a bedroom.

When we sleep our brains go through various cycles, the slowest of which is the delta rhythm of about 1 Hz, which takes place during dreamless sleep. The implication of EM fields of 40-50 Hz hammering on our skulls for eight hours continually is disturbing, even without taking into account our cars, machines, workplaces and other rooms in the house used during the day.

There are also natural Schumann waves emanating from the Earth and resonating precisely with the hippocampus in the mammalian brain. These waves and our connection with them are vital for our health to such an extent that spacecraft need to carry Schumann wave-generators for the astronauts.

Concerns about any interference with these - and other - natural rhythms in our bodies are rapidly on the increase, with a corresponding growth in literature on the subject and devices to remedy the situation.

The latter are particularly interesting, because researchers are having to come up with such strange answers to deal with the onslaught of EM pollution that the devices seem more esoteric than anything we looked at in the previous chapter. Science and mysticism are having to become bedfellows.

A popular example of this would be how people often place quartz crystals near their computers. One person I know puts one on top of her electricity meter - the crystal goes dark after a few years, which is when she replaces it. The piezo-electric qualities of quartz (electricity produced through physical pressure) are known but the use of crystal to protect oneself from the effects of EM stress requires an intuitive leap that many are likely to be uncomfortable with.

Yet the torrent of devices coming on the market today seem just as likely to fuse our logic-circuits: Vortex Units, anti-EMF pendants, BioShields, to name but a few. A recurring principle behind many of them is to boost our immune systems, something that can be also partially achieved through healthy eating and food supplements. The trouble here is that we are in such unknown territory it gives ample room for those with mercenary tendencies to cash in on our ignorance. It's necessary to do one's own homework in this regard and to satisfy oneself either through studying the literature accompanying these devices or through the personal recommendation of friends. Mainstream science is not likely to endorse any of these devices, even when scientists are involved with their development.

Electricity is of the Fire element in Feng Shui: we have effectively harnessed and wrapped lightning around our rooms. This is not a restful situation! One person complained to me of a quickening of her heart, accompanied by short, shallow breathing whenever she lay down on a couch for a siesta in her sitting room. I had come across cases of asthma, eczema, insomnia and hyperactivity in connection with EM stress but this seemed different. I checked the EM field and it was low. I asked her what was underneath the room. This turned out to be a cellar with a storage freezer exactly beneath the couch. After moving the freezer, she rested fine on the couch, after several years of not doing so. The effect of this 'Fire' was coming through a thick stone floor yet didn't register on the field meter. This is in keeping with Alan Hall's research on the vortices around electrical equipment and relates also to Schauberger's theories. TV's and other electrical equipment seem to affect what is directly above and below quite considerably. So, VDU's and TV's are not only frying our retina in front, they also give off large EM fields behind - something of concern when looking at rows of computers in schools - and disruptive fields of life-energy above and below.

With TV there is also a problem in how it is often given pride of place in sitting rooms: this is a way of allowing the ch'i of a machine to dominate human ch'i. The solution is to have the TV available for when you need it but not in the best position of the room - you or your guests should have that! Often the best place for the TV is somewhere along the same wall as the main door into the room. This means you are in the superior position, can see both the TV and the door and not have your back exposed to unknown influences entering the room. If the TV can be in a cupboard with its doors closed when not needed, that is excellent; otherwise, put a cloth over it. Make people your priority - real ones! And don't sleep or sit above or below a TV.

As well as the effects of EM fields from electrical equipment, there can also be a depressive atmosphere for other reasons, something particularly noticeable in offices. One factor is the proliferation of positive ions. This is easily counteracted through the presence of an ioniser or, even better sometimes, an indoor fountain. The latter can create negative ions, have a soothing effect on people and also activate particular areas of a room, such as the Fortunate Blessings/Wealth area - the far left or South-East corner, depending which Feng Shui system you prefer.

Action

Do anything you can to reduce the EM fields in your environment. Consult an open-minded electrician, talk about extra insulation, ducting, a master-switch to cut off the ring mains in your bedroom when you go to sleep (cheaper than a demand switch) - ask them for advice. If it's too late then second choice would be to place amethyst nearby. The crystal-refined EM fields can provide a real boost for your dream life when you're asleep, so be warned!

Poison Air

Another important factor is known collectively as 'Volatile Organic Compounds'. Feng Shui practitioners, space scientists and Natural House builders should all be equally aware of this issue. VOC's are caused by the interaction of machines, body odours, cosmetics and outside influences. They can result in the random breakdown of equipment - and of people. This is particularly evident in studies of sick building syndrome. The answer of how to deal with VOC's came from a scientist, Bill Wolverton, when studying the spacecraft air of Skylab missions. Wolverton identified fifty plants that can recycle VOC's, making the air healthier for humans.

These include, in approximate order, beginning with the most generally efficient:

Areca Palm	(Chrysalidocarpus lutescens)
Lady Palm	(Rhapis excelsa)
Bamboo Palm	(Chamaedorea seifrizii)
Rubber Plant	(Ficus robusta)
Dracaena 'Janet Craig'	(Dracaena deremensis "Janet Craig")
English Ivy	(Hedera helix)
Dwarf Date Palm	(Phoenix roebelenii)
Ficus Alii	(Ficus macleilandii "Alii")
Boston Fern	(Nephrolepsis exaltata "Bostoniensis")
Peace Lily	(Spathiphyllum sp.)

Usually I suggest a minimum of one plant per machine - but if the machine is a photocopier it's best to get it out of the room, preferably in a corridor or a room to itself.

Dirty Water

Plumbing relates to the Water element, obviously, and this is often neglected by people investigating the Feng Shui of a building. In one place I worked on all the natural water was clogged, dirty and accumulating underneath, causing geopathic stress. Not only was this paralleled by extensive difficulties with the plumbing but also with qualities associated with the Water element, such as femininity and intuition.

The sewage system can be a major source of geopathic stress as well, particularly if the sewage is coming from somebody else. Clients of mine had financial problems when they moved into a house, where later it was revealed there was a sewage pipe from the neighbour conjoining with theirs underneath the Wealth area of their house. Another client had a plethora of problems. The sewage pipe was a main conduit for the street and it acted as a subterranean echo of a three-door alignment above, one of the worst perpetrators of killing ch'i. To make matters worse this part of the house was the White Tiger part; something appropriate for the garage which was above the pipe also, but with all the factors put together the Tiger had become uncontrollable and dominant. Before my visit the whole dynamic of the family focused on the kitchen for eating, studying, meeting with friends etc; so part of the answer was to enhance the other side of the house, which up till then had been rarely used, and to limit the kitchen to cooking only. There was an immediate and immense improvement - the solution was imperfect as the problem lay in the foundations of the house itself, but it gave enough survival-space and time until a new house was found.

It's worth getting to know where your Water comes from in your area, knowing its quality and how it moves around your house; and also your sewage system and its placement in your home. It may not be pretty, but it's there, it's real and it's affecting you.

Action:

It's not actually possible to give a panacea for working with any adverse effects from a misplaced sewage system as every case is unique, but as a rough guide you can think of it as a source of potential geopathic stress and try using amethyst crystals in rooms that are affected. Outside drains allow ch'i to leave the site too quickly; so on top of drain covers place earthenware pots with plants that have no thorns or sharp leaves.

Crystals to deal with sewage, plants recommended by a NASA scientist, otherworldly devices to enhance natural rhythms... It's no surprise that adherents to either mystical or scientific disciplines are feeling uncomfortable, for they are only just getting to know each other and the resultant hybrids are rather unusual. We are indeed living in interesting times.

Yet dealing with indoor pollution can result also in very mundane and familiar procedures. To combat the amount of lead we are bringing into our homes and onto our carpets, wiping our feet on a good doormat reduces the risk to a sixth of what it would be normally, according to studies in the States. Even better, removing one's shoes when entering reduces the amount of lead and other toxic substances coming in to at least a tenth of what would normally find its way in. In numerous cultures removing one's shoes on entering a house is simply customary.

Vnder The Sun

While I would never insist on the style of any one culture more than any other, it is often the Japanese who strike me as having succeeded the most (comparatively) in merging the old with the new, and the 'natural' with the 'man-made'. This is not simply because of the innate discipline of Japanese culture, but also because of the significance associated with simple acts. The presence of a leaf or a twig in a room in a small Tokyo flat may seem silly to a Westerner, but with a Japanese consciousness that small object represents Nature in all its glory. A friend of mine trying to learn ikebana - Japanese flower arranging - kept getting admonished by the woman teaching him for doing it wrong even though he copied her arrangements precisely. It took months before he did it with correct awareness, which is when he realised what she had meant all this time.

In Japan very few people actually practise Zen but its pervasiveness is inescapable, influencing every aspect of daily life: the same awareness applied to ikebana can also be applied to the design of electrical circuitry.

There is also a reverence for the past in Japan, partly expressed in the indigenous Shinto religion, but generally, like Zen, it is simply there. Hatsuyume is the name for the first dream of the New Year, that is on the night of the 1st of January or the morning of the 2nd. It is meant to be a dream of important significance, of which the most fortuitous is one of Mount Fuji. This connection with the sacred Earth has parallels elsewhere, such as with the Kikuyu in Africa who revere the mountain Kere-Nyaga, which got characteristically misunderstood by Europeans as 'Kenya'. This sort of connection is not with the past but very much the present - the Earth, which sustains us, in our particular areas, here and now.

In Helston, Cornwall, there is an annual celebration in early May known as the Furry or Floral Dance. It is a tradition undeniably pagan, its roots going far back in time. The celebrations last all day with a number of dances, the first beginning very early morning. The dances vary, one with adults dressed in ballroom clothes, another very noisy one with green-painted dancers covered with foliage, another with the children of the town. All the dances involve a procession winding through the streets. It is an emotive experience which weaves an invisible web between the inhabitants. Tourists come from afar to watch though - as implied earlier - it would be far better if everyone had something similar in their own towns.

Furry Dance, Helston, Cornwall

'This will go onward the same,' Thomas Hardy wrote of rural ways. Ironically, in this case the Furry or Floral Dance has managed to retain its roots by way of constant evolution and change.

Ultimately none of this has anything to do with the past, with tradition or even religion. May Day celebrations are worldwide, even if the actual day varies. In Japan, for instance, May 2nd is understood to be the crucial 88th day from the first day of Spring. In Helston the Furry Dance is usually celebrated on the 8th May, the Feast of the Apparition of St Michael the Archangel, Helston's patron saint. (One recalls also the alignment of the nearby St Michael Line with sunrise on May 1st.) The strength of the Furry Dance is partly through its adaptability, the participants' willingness to constantly update and refresh the ceremonies yet still retaining its original spirit - performers in the Hal-An-Tol dance dress as Robin Hood and His Merrie Men, a popular aspect of the pagan Green Man and his entourage.

Similar festivals also recur in various parts of the world, with respect to their seasonal variations. Most cultures around Autumn-time have a version of All Hallows Eve or Halloween: in Japan known as ohigan, a time to visit the graves of one's ancestors, in Mexico as Dia del Muerte, the Day of the Dead. The dates vary, but the principle remains the same: a connection with yearly cycles, with Nature and, by implication, that which lies beyond.

The modern mind now finds itself in a corner, forced to seek wisdom from the old ways, actually from our elders - and I would include as 'elders' those mentioned at the beginning of this book, practitioners of various healing arts and experienced builders. This takes considerable humility for the desire has been to dominate rather than understand - with, as a result, entire cultures eradicated, species made extinct and the whole Earth put on the brink of destruction for almost a century.

With the benefit of both hindsight and new ways of understanding, the best can be selected globally from the past and from the future. Like the ancient symbol of ouroboros, a snake eating its tail, we can only move forward by being honest with what's behind us. Or like a medicine wheel or stone circle, the cycle is perpetual, it doesn't go anywhere.

It's just there.

Related Reading

Architecture

How Buildings Learn	Stewart Brand	(Phoenix)
A Pattern Language	Christopher Alexander et al	(OUP)
Places of the Soul	Christopher Day	(Thorsons)

General

Autogeddon	Heathcote Williams	(Cape)
The Last Hours of Ancient Sunlight		
	Thom Hartmann	(Three Rivers)
Living Water: Viktor Schauberger and the Secrets of Natural Energy		
	Olof Alexandersson	(Gateway)
The Lost Continent	Bill Bryson	(Black Swan)

Healthy Houses

Eco-Friendly Plants	Bill Wolverton	(Penguin)
The Healthy House	Sydney and Joan Baggs	(HarperCollins)
Killing Fields In The Home	Alasdair and Jean Philips	(Green Audit)
Safe As Houses?	Cowan/Girdlestone	(Gateway)
Water, Electricity and Health	Alan Hall	(Hawthorn)

Glossary

Terms as used in this book.

Ba-gua   Yin-yang symbol combined with an octagon, reflecting eight life-situations.

Barrow   An artificial hill; an ancient grave-mound.

Black Stream   An extremely unhealthy ley line

Black Tortoise   Back of the house. Yin. Nurture and mystery. North.

Ch'i   Energy, life-force.

Cutting ch'i   Harmful ch'i caused by corners of furniture and of walls.

Dragon heart   Important point where many paths of ch'i meet; often a hill in a predominantly flat landscape.

Dragon line   A predominantly yang path of ch'i; also, popularly, any path of ch'i or ley line

Green Dragon   Left side of the building as you stand at the main door, facing outwards. Strong yang. Protection and wisdom. East.

Killing ch'i   Ch'i which flows too fast in a straight line.

Ley   Term used by some dowsers to describe a straight line of yang energy.

Ley line   Popular term used to denote an approximate alignment between important - usually ancient - sites.

Lung mei   Paths of ch'i; literally 'dragon veins'; 'ley lines' in the West.

Red Phoenix   Front of the house, 'the world'. Yang. Joy and luck. South.

Sha   'The life-taking breath'; destructive, unhealthy ch'i - often encouraged by straight lines, stagnant water and untidiness.

Superior Position Using the four animals (Red Phoenix etc) in an interior role, such as a desk or a bed. The Black Tortoise, for instance, is usually in the form of a wall behind where you sit or sleep. The Superior Position is also where you can see the door but are not in its direct flow of ch'i.

Tiger line   A predominantly yin path of ch'i

Tumulus   An artificial mound of earth

White Tiger   Right side of the building as you stand at the main door, facing outwards. Strong yin. Unpredictability, danger. West.

Yang   Active, creative energy eg bright light.

Yin   Passive, receptive energy eg darkness.

Additional Sources

Battle of Camelot   The Guardian   15 Dec 1992

Chemical Warfare at Work   New Scientist   21 June 1997

The Dangers of EMF Radiation   Steve Gamble MGCP   (Apolenus Press)

Devon Ghosts   Theo Brown

Earth To Earth   John Cornwell   (Penguin)

Everyday Exposure to Toxic Pollutants
                                 Scientific American   Feb 1998

A Guide to the Compass   John Cox   (Unpublished MS)

Molecules   P. W. Atkins   (Scientific American)

Phenomena   Fortean Times

Secret Teachings in the Art of Japanese Gardens
                                 David A. Slawson   (Kodansha)

The Symbolism of the Stupa   Adrian Snodgrass   (Motilal Banarsidass)

Tao Te Ching   Gia-Fu Feng &   (Wildwood)
                                 Jane English

Printed in the United Kingdom
by Lightning Source UK Ltd.
100874UKS00003B/4-51